THE COINCIDENCE OF BIRTH

A Collection of Short Stories

TY KEENUM

TY KEENUM
Published by Sandy Springs Press
www.sandyspringspress.com

Printed Worldwide
First Printing 2023
First Edition 2023

10 9 8 7 6 5 4 3 2 1

ISBN: 979-8-9862877-5-1 (eBook)
ISBN:979-8-9862877-6-8 (Paperback)
ISBN:979-8-9862877-7-5 (Hardcover)

Editor: Lila LaBine
Cover Design by GetCovers.com
Follow Ty Keenum online http://www.tykeenum.com

THE COINCIDENCE
OF BIRTH

Dedicated to my wife Karen who makes all things possible,

and to the memory of Bill King, a poet

Table of Contents

INTRODUCTION

I began thinking about some of these short stories back in the 80s in Dallas, Texas. I was a jogger then and I wondered about what would happen if I slipped into a drainage ditch and the only pedestrian traffic was a paperboy. Would he help? I was into Stephen King at the time and thought that the paperboy's perspective might be interesting.

That unknowable puzzle led to a way of analyzing other human interactions as to what coincidences in birth, and life, would influence my relationship with a particular person. Defining these coincidences, these intersections of commonality were recorded in my memories and used as a basis for my writing.

These stories include autobiographical tales that begin in North Carolina and continued in my assorted wanderings throughout the south. The names have all been changed to protect the less than innocent, but like they say, "you know who you are."

The stories are not arranged in chronological order, but as they came to me. Obviously "The Paperboy" is the oldest and had to come first.

It seemed fitting that his growth should become a part of the final story, "Coincidence." I hope you enjoy his journey and the snippets taken from the other time travelers detailed here.

THE PAPERBOY

The prepubescent boy pushes as hard on the pedals of his bike as he can. Finally, in frustration, he gives up. The hill has won the battle again. He steps off his bike and walks it the balance of the way to the peak of the asphalt road. He leans the bike against the wooden post used as a street marker. "Private Drive" reads the sign facing the paperboy. "Hilltop Drive" reads the obverse side.

Hilltop Drive was developed as a compromise between the town council and the town's wealthiest resident, Mr. E.J. Green. The owner of the highest ground for miles around felt that the little municipality should provide a road and services to the site he had selected for his mansion. The city suggested that they could build a road traversing the elevation if it was opened to other home sites. A deal was struck with the magnate that left Mr. Green responsible for the last two hundred yards or so of the drive to his house. The taxpayers would be paying for the mile and a half of frontage road that led to the drive. The prospect of future increased property taxes had swayed some members of the town council. Mr. Green's puppets on the council had provided the remainder of the votes needed for the unanimous decision.

The paperboy quickly decides that the thrill of riding the bike back down the hill of the private drive will not compensate for the struggle involved in pushing the bike to the top. The bike with its double saddlebags loaded with newspapers is just too much on a day that started far too early for a young boy.

Grabbing a single rolled paper, the boy trudges toward the gate that is two hundred yards away up a 30 percent grade. The wrought-iron gate guards the Italian-style mansion positioned on the most elevated property in the county. The first twenty yards or so are punctuated by every curse word the paperboy has ever heard. After a while, the curse words become concatenated into subjects, verbs, and adverbs that no longer make sense, even to the boy. He is venting in the only way he knows how. Eventually his labored breathing discontinues his cursing.

As he pushes his legs harder to compensate for the increased incline, he remembers his one visit inside the gate of the mansion.

The meeting came about as an attempt to collect the customer's four-month outstanding bill. The paper boy's dad drove the boy to the gate to offer support. After a terse interchange over the gate's intercom, the owner himself buzzed the gate open. The scion met the father and son at the front door. The paperboy was astonished that Mr. Green was not much taller than him, and far shorter than his dad. Apparently, Mr. Green noticed the size differential as well because his tone went from intercom pit bull to parlor lapdog.

The father and son were ushered into a room that looked as if it had been transported from an eighteenth-century palace. While there were modern conveniences, the furniture and paintings looked museum old. An odd dusty, musty smell threatened to send the boy into a sneezing fit. Even the carpets looked as though they once bore the weight of knights and ladies.

"Must take quite a staff to keep this place dusted," the dad remarked.

"I live alone," Mr. Green replied. "I have a crew that comes out once a week for the household chores. Same with the yard. I find it to be far more cost-effective to contract for labor rather than to hire employees."

As he walked to a small desk that's value was higher than the dad's annual salary, the defaulter added, "I value my privacy highly, and the thought of someone else sharing my things is abhorrent to me."

While Mr. Green wrote the check for the four months in arrears and two more in advance, he tried to offer excuses for why his bills were always tardy. Sensing an advantage, the paperboy's dad proposed placing a delivery box on the street marker to allow his son to pursue his route more efficiently. Mr. Green would hear none of it. After all, he was "already compromising" by walking to his gate to gather the paper deposited there. To further emphasize his point, he addressed the paper boy directly. "When the task is hard, you work harder. No more excuses!"

No number of compromises offered by the boy's dad would persuade Mr. Green. The meeting was terminated when Mr. Green threatened to call a friend of his at the paper to have the boy fired. Knowing how much his family needed the money, the boy quickly broke his silence and ended the conversation. "Don't worry, Dad, I've got this. I'll get the paper to the gate."

Mr. Green smiled, ushered the pair out the castle-like door, and then watched the father and son exit through the gate. The paperboy was aware that he was being watched. He looked back and could see Mr. Green staring at them from the floor-to-ceiling windows in the main room. *Probably thinks we're going to steal a blade of grass or something,* the boy thought at the time.

Now the boy is in the home stretch of his challenge, only twenty more yards to go. Even though it is cool for this time of year, the boy is sweating. He takes off the flannel shirt he is wearing above his Atlanta Braves T-shirt and ties it around his waist. His umber skin is glistening with perspiration, and he wipes the sweat from his eyebrows with the pointer finger of his hand in a motion like windshield wipers. He shoves the paper in the conical box open at both ends and exhales a deep sigh.

"There you go, you sorry so and so," he says aloud as he wonders if the gate intercom works without pushing the button. He bends deep at the waist to catch his breath and to surreptitiously check to see if the "old so and so" is watching him from somewhere. Rejuvenated, he begins his trek back down the hill. Fast walking, nearly running because of the pitch of the driveway, he is back at his bike in no time.

What he sees confuses him. A cell phone lies on the ground near the front wheel of his bike, which is now on its side, not propped against the signpost as before. He decides not to pick up the cell phone, figuring that the person who lost it would be retracing their steps until they found it. He begins picking up the spilled papers from his saddlebags.

As he picks up the last one, he thinks he hears a faint sound coming from the ditch that is cut from the hill perpendicular behind the signpost. One drainage ditch runs down the private road and is joined at a ninety-degree angle by the ditch running beside the main road. They both join in a culvert that runs under the "private road" to the ditch on the other side. The concrete culvert that carries the confluence of runoff water is about six feet below ground level. The paperboy determines that it must be here that the sound is coming from.

Stepping as close to the edge as he can, the paperboy looks down into the ditch and is dumbfounded by what he sees. At the bottom of the ditch lies Mr. Green on his back. As eye-catching as his garb is the ridiculous angle at which his right leg is turned. The top of the tableau is a brightly colored bicycle helmet encapsulating what is probably a concussed brain. The bottom of the scene is marked by Rollerblades, one straight and one at an almost parallel angle to the body. In between is a mishmash of pads and bands and socks and shirts and shorts in coordinated colors. Some of the colors are starting to change to a deeper maroon.

Seeing the paperboy above him, Mr. Green looks directly into his eyes. "Help me."

The paperboy backs away from Mr. Green's line of sight. While the scene is ghastly, it isn't the blood that is giving the boy pause. He looks about and tries to deconstruct the scene of the accident. Raised on a healthy dose of *Hardy Boys* mysteries, it doesn't take long for the boy to envision a scene of Mr. Green rollerblading down the street and tripping over the boy's bike. The bike that he had left leaning against the street marker.

Maybe he was videoing himself on his phone and not paying attention to where he was skating, the boy speculates. *That would explain why his phone is up top and he's at the bottom.*

After solving the accident scene to his satisfaction, the boy picks up the cell phone. His attempt to dial 911 is rebuffed by the phone's security. The boy walks back to the edge of the culvert and looks down at the broken man below. "What's your phone's security code?"

"What, what?" The question seems to rouse Mr. Green. "I'm not going to tell you my security code. You bring the phone down here to me."

The boy surveys the sheer drop-off and replies, "If I try to get to you, I could get hurt too, and then where would we be?"

Mr. Green grimaces. "Fine. Use your cell phone and call 911. I think I might have internal injuries."

"Don't have one," the boy replies.

"What do you mean you don't have one? Everyone has one. What kind of a parent would send a child out delivering papers without a cell phone? That's child abuse," Mr. Green declares.

The outburst visibly taxes the casualty as he seems to sink even lower in the ditch. The boy peers over the edge and glares at the impudent man who criticized his parents so easily.

"Yeah, well, what do you know?" the boy yells at Mr. Green.

Mr. Green does not respond. The boy can't tell whether the old man is still breathing. Turning to look back at his bicycle and the 127 undelivered papers, it occurs to the boy that Mr. Green might think his bicycle was the cause of the accident.

Oh my god, the boy thinks. *What if that old so and so decides the accident is my fault? What if he comes after Daddy to pay his hospital bills? That'll wreck us.*

The boy walks in circles for a couple of minutes, listening to the angels on each shoulder before hearing the faint "Help" coming from the ditch again.

"Is help coming?" implores Mr. Green.

"First I've got to know that you're not going to blame me for your accident," replies the boy.

"Blame you? Blame you?" the millionaire asks as he raises himself up on one elbow. "Of course I blame you! You left your damn bike in the middle of the street!"

The exertion causes the old man to lie flat on his back again. "Now, are you going to bring me my phone, or are you going to ride to the next house and get me help?"

The paperboy looks down at his tormenter and sees that the maroon color now covers almost all of the man's right side.

"Here, you call," the boy says as he pitches the cell phone at the man.

His aim is true, and he hits Mr. Green squarely in the chest. The phone bounces and lands in a rock outcropping about three feet from the supine rollerblader. Mr. Green reaches in the direction of the phone but stops and screams in pain.

"You've got to help me. It's too hard to reach," implores the stricken man.

"When the task is hard, you work harder. No more excuses!" the boy replies as he turns to complete his paper route. Checking his watch, the boy calculates he is at least fifteen minutes behind schedule. He goes down the mountain at breakneck speed in an attempt to not be late for the school bell. With each paper he delivers, the memory of the old man at the bottom of the ditch grows dimmer. Now it was just man—boy—against machine. Could he possibly deliver the rest of his papers before being counted tardy?

Inwardly he calls for the strength that he has named "Beast Mode." He imagines himself to be the Hulk with unlimited strength as he pushes harder and harder against the bicycle's pedals. The papers fly from his hand with the accuracy born from hundreds of repetitions. Like a champion cyclist entering Paris on the last day of the Tour de France, he enters the school driveway with his arms raised high above his head.

The bell is still clanging when he slips his bike into the rack and locks the wheel with a combination lock. The boy slides into his seat, thanking the gods one more time that his last name begins with a *W*.

"James Washington?" the teacher calls.

"Here," James responds, breathing a sigh of relief.

RICH

The walk from the Guilford County Jail to the Merchandise Mart in High Point was a short one. The *Mutt and Jeff* pair walked as briskly as the smaller man could keep up.

"What the hell, man? I mean really, what the hell?" the taller man called back over his shoulder.

The smaller man huffed out his answer. "I know man. It's just me, it's all on me."

The pair entered the main building of the "largest furnishings industry trade show in the world" along with the hundreds of potential customers. Throngs of well-dressed people were queued in front of registration booths that would check their credentials and issue a "Vendor" or "Guest" pass as the case indicated. This group of early arrivals was just a portion of the estimated seventy thousand or so industry people who flocked to the tiny hamlet twice a year for the expositions. They all seemed to be vying for a spot on the max-to-capacity elevators.

"Let's take the stairs," suggested the man labeled "Rich Mobley" on his vendor's pass.

"Let's not," answered his friend, Ted Kiner. "If you start sweating, it's going to knock the flies out of the air, not to mention what it will do to your customers and the rest of us. Our best shot is to see how much we can get you cleaned up before your customers come in. I'm sure somebody has Listerine and mints."

The pair shoved into the elevator and rode cheek by jowl to the fourth floor. As the door opened, the pair split up. Rich went to the men's room to freshen up with whatever tools were available. Ted navigated his way to the showroom to see what resources the other salespeople might have that would aid in Rich's rehabilitation.

The NL&A showroom was already abuzz with salespeople dusting, vacuuming, and double-checking prices. A pair of salespersons, interior designers in a previous incarnation, were setting the window vignettes that displayed the pictures, lamps, and other accessory items that constituted the showroom's raison d'être.

"Is he all right?" Newton Laine, the owner, asked.

"He's fine, considering. There's no visible bruising," Ted replied.

The sales force had gathered about the two men.

"I need Listerine, mints, cologne, a clean shirt, whatever anybody has that will cover the smell of the drunk tank."

Gathering the salespeople's offerings, he put them in his coat pockets and looked at his watch. "Rich's appointment with the Kaines is for nine, and it's ten till now. I'll have him back in time if I can, but if not, someone will need to schmooze them until we get back."

"We'll handle it," Newton replied. "This could be Rich's market. We won't let them get away."

Could be Rich's market, thought Ted as he headed for the men's room. *Understatement of the year.*

The Kaines' forty-four stores scattered across Florida were a furniture juggernaut. The Kaines had enough buying power to make the entire showroom's market. Getting on the Kaines' Preferred Vendor list could set a salesperson up for life.

Pushing open the door to the men's room, Ted found Rich standing bare-chested in front of the hand dryer. His shirt was being rubbed back and forth between his hands under the dryer. Apparently, Rich had decided to wash the shirt using hand soap and was now trying to get it dry enough to wear. Every so often he punched the dryer to keep it going. Other hygienically conscious users of the facility were using paper towels or their clothes to dry their hands rather than challenging the half-naked man commandeering the hand dryer.

"It's good that the stubble look is in vogue now," said Ted. "You might carry off the idea that you meant to not shave today."

"Yeah," Rich grunted.

The hirsute man examined his face in the mirror. If Rich had a "spirit animal," it was the Florida black bear. The round hairy body belied the unusual strength of the man. When not bound to the constraints of his job, the hungover salesperson regularly did three-tank dives in the Florida Keys. Prior to coming to this market, Rich had scored dozens of lobsters off the Big Pine Key. He had packed the spiny lobsters in an ice chest, along with several red-tailed snappers he had speared, to share with the group. A spectacular feast was coming for the group if they could keep the chef out of trouble.

Ted waited for Rich to put his shirt back on before handing him the Listerine. "I'd gargle really, really good, and then we can follow it up with mints for the rest of the day."

Rich gargled loudly, as if the ferocity of the exercise would exorcise the underlying problem. Pushing his hair with his hands, he attempted to make a part. He slid the pre-tied necktie around his neck and snapped his collar down over it. "I don't know where my coat is. I've got an idea, but I'm not sure," he said as he opened the men's room door. "I'll just tell 'em I was so excited about working with them today I left it in the car."

The pair turned the corner into the showroom and walked directly into the Kaines 'contingent. The showroom's number one producer and only natural born salesperson was front and center.

~ ~ ~

Two and a half hours later, Rich held purchase orders for three accessory lines totaling over two million dollars. Rich had landed the whale. When confirmed, the orders would constitute half of the showroom's total market sales. At a 5 percent commission rate, Rich had made his year, and the year was only one-third done. It was April, and if past trends held true, the fall market in October would be an even bigger windfall for the young Florida native.

Convinced that he was done for the day, Rich left before lunch for the motel on the outskirts of Greensboro. The entire crew implored him to get a shower and take a nap.

~ ~ ~

Ted rolled up on the motel about half past six that evening. Unsure whether his roommate would want dinner that night, he decided to give Rich the opportunity to choose for himself. The rest of the group would be commandeering a popular steakhouse in Greensboro to celebrate the success of the day.

As he stepped out of the car, he was nearly dropped to his knees by the sight of one of their boss's stepdaughters leaving his and Rich's room. He hoped it was the eldest, who was eighteen, but he was quite sure it was Wendy, the fifteen-year-old. Praying that it was innocent, but knowing that it probably wasn't, Ted opened the door.

Rich was sitting on the edge of his bed in his full glory. "Hey, Bubba."

"I don't want to know," Ted answered. "If I know, I'm going to wind up having to lie to somebody, and I don't want to be in that position."

"OK," Rich replied nonchalantly. "What's up?"

"We're all going to the steakhouse in Greensboro if you're interested," Ted answered.

"Sure, sure. I've built up quite an appetite," Rich offered as he headed for the shower.

"I told you, I don't want to hear about it," Ted answered as he turned on the TV to catch the local news.

~ ~ ~

The drive to the steakhouse was silent. The rest of the group was waiting at a large table reserved days before. The scene was chaotic. The restaurant was filled beyond capacity and serviced by employees that seemed to be called into work just twice a year by the markets.

During markets, the unemployment figures in the High Point–Winston-Salem–Greensboro tri-cities was –0.10. Any warm body that was ambulatory was called into service. Local homeowners planned their vacations in anticipation of renting their homes to desperate furniture buyers. Those market goers lucky enough to be staying in a hotel or motel room secured their next stay with a deposit at checkout. As the local saying went, rooms were "scarcer than hen's teeth."

The meal went as well as could be expected with the usual number of mistaken orders, undercooked steaks, and extraordinary waits. Newton made a big show of grabbing the check, which made the meal taste a little sweeter.

Ted raised his glass to Newton's end of the table to acknowledge Newton's gesture. *With his 10 percent cut of Rich's orders and the balance of whatever the showroom took in today, he can well afford it.*

Ted purposely avoided looking at Marsha, Newton's wife. The sound of her unbridled laughter told Ted that Marsha had joined Newton well down in their cups. "*Clearly, she doesn't know what's going on with her daughters, or doesn't care,* he thought as the group rose to leave. Hopeful of escaping the night without a confrontation, he tugged at Rich's sleeve, and they were the first to the parking lot and away. The drive back to the motel was silent.

Ted waited until Rich was down to his boxers and propped up in his bed channel surfing before beginning.

"You made one hundred thousand dollars today," Ted began. "And you potentially threw away one hundred thousand dollars. And, man, I just don't understand."

"Ain't your business to understand," Rich bristled, and dropped the remote. "You can be my friend or not, but nobody needs to even try to understand me."

"OK, try to understand me," Ted replied. "Bailing you out is no fun, but maybe that's just one of those things that can come up in a friendship. This other thing, whatever it is, is not a 'bail you out' situation. It's a 'bury you under the jail' kind of situation. It's a 'throw away the key' situation. It's a 'branded for life when you get out, if you ever get out' situation."

Ted paused to look Rich straight in the eyes. "I don't understand why a guy as smart as you doesn't see that you're putting both of us in a horrible situation. Even if it was the older sister, it's a problem, but I'm fairly sure it was Wendy, the crazy one. And that's like pouring gasoline all over yourself and handing her a box of matches."

Ted reached into the Coleman ice chest and pulled out a Diet Coke. He raised his eyebrows to Rich.

Rich responded, "Naw."

Ted popped the top, sipped, and said, "I mean, I've only been with the company for six months, and I've heard stuff, but this is just crazy."

"Heard stuff, what kind of stuff," Rich asked as he slid his legs over the side of the bed. "Did you hear about where I grew up, where I went to high school?"

"Well, I heard you grew up in Panama City mostly. Your dad is a Cuban exile and had three or four wives and a bunch of girlfriends. You've got four brothers and one sister, and you've all got different moms. Your dad ran motels and restaurants, and all the kids had to help because he didn't like paying people. I heard that's where you learned to cook and that you took shifts in a restaurant when you were twelve. I didn't hear anything about a proclivity for underage girls."

"Did you hear I went to high school at Raiford?" Rich was standing now, and the room was beginning to feel very crowded. "Did the little birds tell you that?"

Ted took a few seconds to process what he thought he was hearing. The only reference he had ever heard for Raiford was the Florida state prison. *Maybe there's a high school in the town for the kids of the prison's employees?*

Rich stared intently at Ted. "You figured it out yet? I went to high school in prison."

"You're kidding" was the only response Ted could muster.

"I wish I was," Rich replied. "I can't believe nobody told you." He gave Ted a little twisted grin. "You're sharing a room with a convicted murderer."

Now the room felt really, really small. The room felt as if it had been depressurized; the air seemed to have left the room completely.

"What happened?" Ted asked.

"Me and a couple of my brothers and some other guys had gone up to Deer Point Lake to fish and maybe shoot some turtles. When we got to our spot under the bridge of 77A there were some colored boys already there. We kind of agreed to give each other some space north and south of the bridge, and it worked out fine until nightfall. We were all leaving at the same time, and one of the colored boys said something about my string of fish. I said something back and maybe at some point I called him a nigger, and then it was on."

Rich reached into the Coleman cooler and pulled out a beer. Taking a long draft, he continued the story. "Well, long story short, he whipped my ass. I was fourteen, and I guess he was about eighteen. My brothers or somebody should have jumped in and helped me, but they didn't. They say they let me fight my own battles to make me tough, but I suspect they were scared they'd get whupped too."

Rich took another long pull of the beer. "Anyhow, I'm lying on the side of the road, and the colored boys have all loaded up and are driving off." He sat on the side of the bed and looked down between his feet. "I couldn't just let him go without at least scaring him a little, so I grabbed the rifle and shot at the car. I meant to shoot over it, but I guess bullets drop a little after a distance, and it hit a fella in the back seat. Wasn't even the guy that whipped me. Just some other guy that went out for a day of fishing and got killed for his trouble."

Rich looked up and stared into Ted's soul. "Honest to God, I didn't mean to kill anybody, I just wanted to scare 'em. I wanted them to know they couldn't mess with me. I've been small all my life. I've got older brothers. I was just so sick and tired of being picked on, of taking a beating."

Ted's brain was racing. "But you were just a kid. Raiford is the adult penitentiary. There's no way they should have sent you there."

"Yeah, except between the time I was arrested and the trial, I turned fifteen, and Florida likes to get a head start on getting their problems off the streets. I was tried as an adult and convicted of second-degree manslaughter. They let me out when I turned twenty-one. I don't have a clue what their criteria for evaluating my rehabilitation was."

Rich polished off the beer and reached for another one. "I'm a felon. I can't vote, I can't own a gun, and most importantly, I can't get a job. I lucked into this job, and you're right, I'm probably going to screw myself up."

Ted sorted through the myriad of questions in his mind and decided to pursue the most pressing matter. "Why chase after one of the boss's kids, particularly the one that's underage? I've seen you hook up with all sorts of women. Hell, man, you're married. You could bring your wife to market. A lot of guys do."

"It ain't about that." Rich looked between his feet again. "I was fifteen when I went into prison. I was the fresh meat. Even the guys that ain't queer will take advantage of you in there. You have to tell yourself it's not a sexual thing, that it's about power, it's about being able to dominate someone else while you're being dominated. You 'go along to get along' until finally you're released."

Rich aimed his beer can at the wastepaper basket and scored from six feet. "You try to fill that gap of where you are with where you think you should be. You want to be where you should be, if you hadn't lost a chunk of your life."

He returned to the head of his bed and propped himself up on his pillows. "Then a cute—yes, crazy—fifteen-year-old girl starts flirting with you, and your brain goes back to being fifteen again. I ain't excusing it. I'm just saying that's how it is."

The room was quiet for several minutes.

Ted finally broke the silence. "This is not going to work for me."

"Yeah," Rich replied. "I figured this was where we were going. How about I tell Newton tomorrow I've got a family emergency back home and I'm going to leave early. There's only two more days of market anyway, and I've already paid his mortgage for him, so he shouldn't give me any grief."

"I think that's best," Ted responded. "We can flip for who gets the room for next market. Odd guy has to find other accommodations."

"Whatever," replied Rich, who promptly rolled over onto his side.

In minutes, he was sleeping peacefully. His roommate was not as lucky.

Surviving Love

The only sound heard inside the laboratory from the activation of the blow-off booth was an electric click. As the door from the "BOB" into the anteroom opened, a larger *whoosh* was followed by the clunky sounds of footsteps. The footsteps came from the entity enclosed in a biohazard space suit. Walking into the anteroom the "spaceman" turned and ensured that the inner door of the BOB was closed tightly. For extra measure, he took a fresh roll of duct tape and outlined the seal of the door.

Satisfied that whatever it was that was poisoning the outside was not coming inside, he removed his helmet. He quickly glanced through the glass wall of the anteroom at the form sleeping on the cot in the corner of the laboratory. As quietly as possible, he removed the suit and placed it in the locker on the hooks designed specifically for it. Standing in his T-shirt and boxers, he pulled on his jeans and sweatshirt. If he was lucky, his roommate would not know he had gone out.

He took his repurposed book bag over to the lab's large double sink and began removing cans from it. He wanted to finish his mission as quickly as possible; he hated explaining his actions to his roommate. In near silence, he washed each can in antiseptic soap before placing it on a shelf in the pantry. Whatever had taken the world back to the Stone Age was airborne. Washing cans was perhaps overkill, but they were six months and eight days from the event that had killed the world, and they were still alive. They were still kicking.

The day had started much like any other day for the graduate student. The budding scientist worked in the biochem lab at the state university. He enjoyed his work immensely even if the other members of the research group treated him more as a gofer than a colleague.

On this beautiful bright spring day, he was surprised to see an animal rights group protesting outside the laboratory complex. He was shocked to see the group when it was barely daylight. It was rare for him to see anyone other than security that early. The rest of the research team usually arrived just in time to take an early lunch. As he stopped to sign in at the security desk, a beautiful woman stuck a microphone in his face.

"Do you work here?" she inquired.

"Huh, what, yes," he sputtered, looking away from her face to conceal his shyness. His vision went past Channel 6's latest eye candy to the massively big TV screen on the wall in the waiting area. WWN's *Breaking News* reported that dirty bombs were exploding in all the major metropolitan areas of the world.

"What do you do?" the vision in a cardigan and jeans was asking.

"I, uh," he stammered as they felt the floor rumble beneath them. Looking out the glass front of the building, he saw a mushroom cloud rising with a dust cloud pushing toward them. As the security guard ran toward the front doors, the student grabbed the woman's wrist firmly and pulled her toward the open elevator. Instantly and forever embarrassed, he uttered the words, "Come with me if you want to live."

The woman offered no resistance, and they rode the elevator in silence to the basement. Turning right out of the elevator, the student dragged the reporter as quickly as he could to the biochem lab. He slid his key card through the security slot, and they entered the blow-off booth together.

The high-velocity blow-off system was designed to effectively remove all potentially hazardous materials, including a dirty bomb laced with a neurotoxin or pathogen. The booth was effective not only in removing dust from people but also in cleaning materials brought into the clean zone. A feature that would prove to be lifesaving as time went on.

Within seconds, their bodies were completely clean from any harmful dust that might have reached them from the blast.

"Are we safe here?" asked the woman, who identified herself as Amanda.

"As safe as you can be barring a bomb dropped on the building," the lab tech responded. "I'm Axle."

The reporter took his outstretched hand. "Axl like Axl Rose?"

"Axle like connecting two wheels together for a more efficient means of moving things. My dad was a master mechanic. He thought it would be an effective way to get me interested in engineering. Here, let me show you around," Axle offered as the pair stepped into the laboratory.

"This is what is known as a cleanroom," he said as he waved his arms expansively. "A cleanroom must have less than 35 million particles greater than 0.5 micron per cubic meter and 20 HEPA filtered air changes per hour. So, we're going to be breathing antiseptically clean air for as long as the filters hold out."

He pointed to a row of vented boxes lined along the ceiling all around the room like a tour guide at a museum.

Oh geez, Axle thought. *I just totally nerded out.*

Amanda had moved to one of the stools and started furiously thumbing her cell phone. "There's no bars. I can't get any reception." She waved her phone frantically, her face forming a pout. "How am I going to check in with my station manager and let him know what's going on?"

"We're not really allowed to bring anything into the cleanroom," Axle answered. "But . . . we can check the landline." He walked to the wall-mounted, smooth-faced phone and pressed 9 for an outside line. Dead silence. The internal system appeared to still be up, and he tried the security desk. After ten rings, he hung up.

"The outside line is dead," he said as he pushed the ON phone button for Amanda to confirm for herself. The lack of a dial tone added to their anxieties.

"We can see if the internet is still up," he offered while spinning up one of the computers mounted on carts scattered about. Using the touch keyboard, he was able to access the internet. "Google's still up," he said in an almost reverent tone.

"Move," Amanda said as she used her bottom to scoot Axle from the stool. She typed "www.WWNNews.com" into the computer, and the computer screen revealed a picture of the newsroom morning-show anchors still in their chairs. The usually too animated anchors were slumped over and not moving.

"Oh god!" she exhaled, relinquishing the seat back to Axle. Her eyes widened as she looked at Axle. "This is only temporary right? I mean, I've got plans. Six months at WWN and then on to network. This can't be happening to me, not now."

Axle began searching the internet for any signs of life. His search for the FEMA site was fruitless. It was then that he was forced to reveal a personal secret to Amanda.

Earlier in the year he had Velcroed a USB radio drive under his stool. He didn't see the harm in listening to the broadcast of his alma mater's football team while he worked. Admitting to Amanda that he didn't always play by the rules, he recovered the contraband from its hiding place. Placing the drive in the PC, Axle was able to tune the radio to 640 AM and pick up the Conelrad system.

The relic from the 1950s blared its screeching alert sound, which was followed by the mechanical voice: "This is your Emergency Alert System. The United States is under attack. Remain indoors. Seal your doors and windows. Do not go outside until given the all clear. This station will broadcast updates every fifteen minutes."

"Jesus," remarked Amanda. She grabbed a stool and pulled it next to Axle. "What does all of that mean?"

"It means we're in the safest place we could possibly be," Axle replied while not looking Amanda directly in the face. "I mean, I guess the President and them have a better setup, if they had time to get there. Here, let me check something." He leaned over the keyboard. "The Weather Channel sometimes shows a live shot from up on Windy Hill. That might let us know how bad it is."

The Weather Channel camera showed a scene of death and destruction that made both survivors avert their eyes. The expressways in both directions were totally blocked. Bodies of all sexes, ages, and races were strewn about. Whatever the thin layer of dust was that covered everything in the camera's range, it was apparently instantly fatal. The people who had left their cars to see what the problem was had dropped on the spot.

"I-I-I really need to go to the bathroom," Amanda announced.

And with that, Axle was able to deliver the only good news of the day. "We happen to be one of the few cleanrooms anywhere with a bathroom attached. Here, let me show you."

He escorted her to the unisex bathroom and waited for her at an appropriate distance. He didn't know what to expect, but he knew he didn't want her to try to run out the way she had come in. When she returned, she looked as if all the air had been let out of her sails. Her mascara was streaked down her face, but it didn't diminish her natural beauty. Axle was smitten.

"What now?" Amanda asked as she looked around the lab.

"We await further instructions," Axle replied.

None came.

~ ~ ~

Slipping the last can into the pantry, Axle felt the hairs on the back of his neck stand up. Amanda had slipped up behind him and was now standing six inches away in her underwear. He could see from her reflection in the stainless-steel cabinet that she was glaring at him.

She had taken to wearing just her underwear, or less, after their first month of confinement. In spite of her seductive behavior, they had only been intimate once. Axle knew it had been a colossal failure almost immediately. If any doubt remained, it had been dashed as Amanda delighted in elaborating at length about his lack of charisma. Repeatedly. They never attempted it again.

It was maddening for Axle to see her parading around seminude. It seemed that she was comfortable with him seeing her in the most personal way but didn't care how he was affected.

"You went out again," Amanda said.

"Had to," Axle answered, slipping further out of her range. "We were running out of that toothpaste you like, and I picked up some other things."

"Last time you said next time you would take me with you," Amanda said as she pressed closer to Axle. "You've lied to me again!"

Axle backed up and walked over to the card table he had secured to use as a dining and game table. Sitting down, he put his head in his hands and waited for the onslaught to finish.

This diatribe included the word *Poindexter*, which he knew Amanda had picked up from the movie *Revenge of the Nerds*. Hoisted on his own petard, Axle laughed to himself and waited for Amanda to run out of steam before attempting to offer a rebuttal.

While she raged, he looked about the room that he had diligently converted into their living quarters. Over time he had secured a TV and DVD player for movies. They had a stereo with stacks of CDs. He had raided the student center of the board games he felt might pique Amanda's interest. He had pilfered books from the library. He started first with the classics and descended to "young adult supernatural" and then to "bodice rippers." For an investigative reporter, Amanda lacked curiosity about literature, which struck Axel as an oxymoron.

Amanda accused him of trying to seduce her through the reading material. While there was still a glimmer of hope there for Axle, he was truly trying to find something that would turn Amanda's focus away from him.

"I don't need you," Amanda was shouting at him now. "I can put on that stupid suit all by myself and find my own cleanroom. Heck, I can walk back home from here. I don't need to stay locked up in here with you ogling me all day long. You even watch me when you think I'm asleep. I've seen you."

Amanda paused to catch her breath.

As he waited for the next verbal assault, Axle admitted to himself that she was right. He did watch her while she was asleep. He watched her all the time. Equally true, she could put on one of the suits and head out on her own. She could walk to wherever she wanted to, but where would that be?

The university was powered by its own 5-megawatt nuclear power plant. Axle had taken a night excursion about a month after the attack, and the city was completely dark. He had expected some light somewhere, maybe even someone flashing an SOS. Nothing. It was pitch black except for the biochem building.

Fortunately, the lab refrigerators allowed them to store leftover meals, to have a cold beer, or glass of wine. Refrigeration out in the world was gone, but here in their little hideout, Axle was able to provide chilled fruit drinks and Diet Pepsis to his tormentor. Although he was deeply, desperately infatuated with Amanda, he did recognize her as his personal intimidator.

The loss of power outside of the university was not the starkest reminder of the day of the attack. Rotting corpses were everywhere. The students protesting for the ethical treatment of animals had dropped right outside the door to the building. Ironically, there were no more animals to take advantage of the feast. No buzzards or crows, no pack of wild dogs or even cats. Whatever was contained in the dust scattered everywhere was deadly to everything.

At first, Axle's scientific curiosity was piqued, and he was excited at the prospect of discovering what was in the dust. Maybe not to find a cure, but a possible explanation. He had even taken a sample jar outside with him. Just as he was about to use a toothbrush to sweep some dust into his sample jar, a voice in his head chastened him. *What's the point?*

After reflecting for a moment, Axle agreed with his inner voice. *What's the point? Do dead people need to know what killed them?*

"I mean it. I'm going to wait for you to go to sleep, and then I'm going to sneak out like you do to me," Amanda said.

Summoning all his courage, Axle replied, "No, you're not, and if you keep threatening me like that, I'm going to chain you to your bed."

"Oh, you'd love that, wouldn't you?" Amanda yelled. "Me all chained to the bed, waiting to do your bidding."

"No, that's the last thing in the world I want," Axle quietly answered. "I just want us to both live as long as we can." He stood and walked to the anteroom. "Everything outside is dead. Dead. There are no disco bars with ladies' nights, there's no spin classes, no book clubs, just death and dust. I know you think I've faked the dozens of pictures I've taken for you. I'm somewhat flattered by the accusation, but you're wrong. They're real. The world is gone."

Axle opened the anteroom door and motioned for Amanda to come over. He pointed at a row of green gas canisters lined along the wall. "When we started here, there were thirteen full canisters. Now there's six. I haven't located any others in my scouting trips. When these are gone, I'll have to rely just on the filters in the suit. I don't know if they're strong enough to repel whatever it is out there."

Axle closed the door to the anteroom and sat back down at the table. "When I go out, I know where I'm going. I'm very efficient in my trips"—he looked directly at Amanda—"and I control my breathing. I'm not breathing like some Valley Girl cheerleader going, 'Oh my god! Oh my god!' I'm conserving our most valuable resource as best I can."

Amanda's face turned into a pout; it was not the first time she had heard the lecture. She sat down opposite him at the card table. "I hate it here, I hate it here, I hate it here. I don't hate you yet, but I'm getting there."

For the first time in their time together, Amanda lowered her guard. She spoke not in the confident voice of a beauty queen, a sixteen-time pageant winner, but as a scared little girl. Forgotten for the moment was the young woman who attained a scholarship to journalism school because of her ability to twirl a baton better than anyone in the tri-state area. She spoke now as Amanda June Humphries from Sparta, a woman whose only strengths were her beauty and her ability to exploit her physical gifts to attain her goals.

"I'm scared," she began. "I'm scared we aren't going to ever get out of here. I'm scared that if we do get out there's nothing left. I'm scared that even if there are people like us scattered about that the world no longer needs me."

She paused to look around. "The world needs you and all the stuff you know. I don't know anything except how to hit my mark and look at the camera with the red light. The world will never need that again."

She bit on her lip, holding back the tears. "I'm scared, and I think I'm jealous of you for being smart, and worried that at some point you'll just see me as an anchor weighing you down. I'm scared that you might see life as being easier without me and want me gone."

Axle reached across the table to put his hand on top of Amanda's. She allowed his touch. "Believe me, that's the last thing I'd ever want. Tell you what," he said as he grasped her hand lightly. "If you really hate it here, how about tomorrow we go out together? On one condition: we do it without supplemental air."

Amanda's eyes filled with tears. "Really? You really mean it this time?"

"Yeah, I mean it." Axle got up and pulled a beer from the refrigerator. "We're going to run out of air before the one-year anniversary. If I die on a scavenging trip, you're not going to survive alone here. We might as well go out together, so to speak."

Amanda smiled for what Axle felt like was the first time since "the day." That night she crawled into bed with him and allowed him to fumble about for as long and often as he wanted. As Axle watched Amanda fall asleep, he knew the plan was foolish. Waiting until the last possible moment to test the respirators was the best course of action. Maybe he would find more air cannisters, maybe the toxin only had a shelf-life of a year, maybe there was some other way to create the smile that beamed from Amanda's face.

~ ~ ~

The next morning, Amanda was up and ready before Axle had cleared the sleep from his eyes. While they dressed in the protective suits, Amanda displayed her nervousness through constant chatter. Axle's nervousness was much deeper, more like trepidation.

As he had promised, they would make the trip without the supplemental oxygen. Only the respirators from their suits would protect them from whatever had poisoned the environment. They took the elevator up to the first floor and walked briskly across the lobby to the glass doors. Maybe it was Amanda's first exposure to sunlight in six months that slowed her steps, or maybe it was negotiating around the prostrate bodies of her former broadcast crew.

As Axle looked back at her, he grinned. The grin was to a certain degree the product of an old joke Axle had just remembered. The joke was about a ninety-year-old man who died in the act of making love. The punch line was "and the undertaker just couldn't get the grin off of his face."

Axle was grinning when he dropped to his knees and then to his face.

HELEN

The Piedmont Prison was constructed and opened in 1924 on the outskirts of town in a suburb known as Woodlands. Designed as a medium-security prison, it took its name from the towering mountain nearby. The inmates incarcerated there were convicted of petty crimes—assault, theft, and some class 4 felonies. Generally speaking, this was not a prison with a dangerous population. The more dangerous characters were shipped off to the state prison.

The inmates that volunteered for work were utilized in the prison laundry or on road crews. The laundry was in a building completely separated from the prison by a large parking lot. The inmates assigned to the laundry were responsible for washing and pressing all the uniforms for the correctional facility, even the uniforms of the officers. The allegations that prison labor supplemented the local laundries for a fee were ever substantiated, even though trucks from the local laundries could be seen in the parking lot every day.

The road crews were primarily responsible for filling potholes and painting lines. They would occasionally do minor repairs if the skill set for the repair was available. If no repairs were assigned, the road crews would spend their time picking up trash.

In 1931, the prison underwent an expansion designed to keep up with the rapid growth of the city nearby. The city needed more road crews, and prison labor was cheap. The original prison remained "open for business" until the state legislation approved funds to build a new one. The new prison was located less than a mile from its predecessor. The proximity allowed the new prison to maintain use of the original laundry facilities. The new Piedmont Prison opened its doors in 1989, promising to keep its charges in a more humane manner.

It was in this new prison that recently certified Registered Nurse Helen Morris applied for and was awarded the position of head nurse. Helen had arrived for the interview in her nurse outfit, "ready to start right now" if called on. She took pride in the fact that she looked at least ten years younger than the age listed on her driver's license. In truth, Helen was just three years short of the mandatory retirement age of sixty-five. Some might have viewed the hire as risky for the prison administration.

On the one hand, the state would not be encumbered by a pension; five years of service was the minimum required to be vested. On the other hand, they were hiring a recent graduate. Could a newly minted nurse possibly be qualified to handle the host of symptoms encountered in a prison? Placing a woman, particularly one in her elder years, in close proximity to criminals could have been viewed as a potential liability for the prison. In the end, Helen's offer to take 10 percent less than the posted starting pay sealed the deal.

Driving back down the narrow state road, the only way in or out of the mountain detention center, Helen was furiously talking to herself. Before reaching the city limits, Helen rationalized, *How they handle that ten percent I'm not getting is not my concern. My concern is getting my Social Security pumped up while I still can.*

As she drove into her driveway, she was greeted from her porch by her sister Edna and daughter Charlotte.

"Did you git it, did you git it?" they yelled in unison, running toward the car as fast as their aged bodies would carry them.

"I got it," Helen replied.

The women joined in a collective hug there in the yard. Extracting herself, Helen walked up the sidewalk to her house. "Let me change out of my uniform and I'll take us all out to eat," she called over her shoulder as she headed into the house.

The welcoming committee was waiting patiently on the porch when she returned. The trio went to a local Greek place that was known for its salads and competitive prices. Helen's daughter was the only one to order dessert. She couldn't resist their baklava.

Helen didn't reveal to the group that she would be working for less than scale. Nor did she give voice to any other misgivings she might have had about working with 120 of society's outcasts. The conversation that evening was light and filled with excitement for her prospects.

An observer of the group would think they were watching three elderly ladies of the same age. Though Edna was eight years younger than Helen, she looked older. Helen's daughter was discernible as the youngest member of the trio, but just barely. They referred to themselves as "the Golden Girls," parodying the popular TV show.

When the check came, there was only one set of hands above the table. Helen placed her credit card on the tray, a kindness that over time had become a tradition. Her sister and daughter murmured quiet thank-yous, but no offer came to share the bill, not even to cover the tip.

~ ~ ~

The first day in a new job can be so overwhelming for some people that they leave and never return. Not so with Helen. She viewed the first group of ten inmates seated in the waiting room outside her door as a positive. When the second group of ten arrived and then the third, Helen felt that she had the most secure job in the prison. After clocking thirty patients, she lost count. She kept her head down and tried to relieve as many ills as possible.

The new head nurse had spent her weekend reading up on the common diseases found in prison. There were the normal diseases found in the general population: high blood pressure, diabetes, arthritis, asthma, and cirrhosis of the liver. Many of the inmates were chronic substance abusers and had done considerable damage to their kidneys and liver before entering the prison system. It was up to Helen to ease their pain and reverse some of those conditions if she could.

Prisons were also hotbeds of infectious diseases like tuberculosis, hepatitis B and C, and sexually transmitted infections. The AIDS virus was running rampant in the world, and no one really knew how to treat it or how it was passed. Helen vowed to always wear a mask and gloves, even though it was not what she considered the best bedside manner. She would have to convey her concern for the patient in her eyes, voice, and words.

Helen worked through her first day of aches and pains without incident. She found only one patient to be sick enough to require a doctor's care. Since it was not a case of immediate care, in which case the patient would have been transferred to the hospital, he was put on the doctor's schedule.

He's on his way to the golf course, Helen thought after watching the doctor dispatch with his cases in record time on that first Friday.

Dr. Hammond was in his late forties but had already peaked in his career. Federal investigations of prescription-pad abuse had led him to become the prison doctor for the surrounding area. While the doctor appeared to be competent, Helen didn't like the way his pupils danced when she looked him in the eye.

~ ~ ~

The week had passed quickly. Dinners were rotated between the Golden Girls each night. Charlotte would leave the sanctity of her basement apartment only to pick up dinner from Wendy's. It was apparent from the exasperation showing on her face that she was glad her turn came only twice a week.

Edna usually prepared something in a slow cooker for her contribution. She would bring the pot next door to Helen's house, and the group would discover together what combinations of meats and vegetables Edna had decided on that day. They would munch on hash while they rehashed Helen's day.

Typically, the local news would be playing in the background while the group ate. There was always a news item that provided Helen the gravitas to pronounce that what she was seeing on TV was just exactly why the prisons were "bustin' at the seams."

"Welfare queens popping out more and more babies so they can get a bigger check is just how these people game the system. They know how the system works, and they make it work for them" was a rejoinder parroted by one or the other at various times in an evening.

The sight of any person of color on the TV seemed to raise the temperature of the group, no matter what the context. Black national figures seemed to turn the group apoplectic. When the local station employed a Black anchor, the group began watching a rival station that was situated sixty miles away. Even though the picture was snowy, it was snowy white.

Shortly after Helen took her job, Charlotte offered to help by running errands for her mom. She wanted to allow her mom to rest on the weekends. Armed with her mom's credit card she went about town buying groceries, picking up the laundry, visiting the home-improvement store, whatever Helen dictated. Helen noticed on her bank statements that Charlotte was giving herself a "fee" for helping her mom, but it went unmentioned.

Helen was sitting on her front porch on one of those restful weekends when a flying ant landed on her arm. Upon closer inspection she determined that the flying ant was a termite. Walking about her house, she could find no funnels, no instances of wood touching the earth. Continuing her search to her sister's house next door, she found a pile of two-by-fours stacked next to Edna's house.

The termite funnels leading upward indicated a widespread infestation.

Edna had no job and a ridiculously small pension. Helen often "loaned" her sibling the money required to remedy her assorted problems. Helen chose not to remind Edna once again what a failure she was when she wrote the check to the exterminator. Her Christian upbringing kept her tongue in check.

That night the Golden Girls watched in horror as the story of the Central Park Jogger broke out on TV. Quick to judge and slow to retract, Helen expounded for the next hour or so on the state of the Union.

"Until somebody comes in and forces these people to be sterilized or something like that, these people are just going to keep breeding. If we don't nip it in the bud, these kinds of things will keep happening to good God-fearing people. Mark my words," she declared as she rose for bed. No rebuttals were offered to her final solution.

Helen often wondered, *How will they survive when I'm gone?* as she waited for sleep to take her. She was not comforted by her mental responses.

I just need to set things up well enough before I go so that they will be able to get by was her nightly mantra as she passed through her conscious state. *They'll run through their inheritance in a week if I don't watch out for them.*

One prisoner, a frail fellow named Lenny, seemed to be in Helen's office at least once a week. He was a "high yellow" with an effeminate persona. Helen suspected that his countenance drew the bullies to him like bees to honey. She had to admit, Lenny was very engaging.

He would start off conversations with "Mizz Helen, have you ever been to . . ." and then listen to Helen's description of the place while she attended to him. On one visit he brought her a little house constructed from chewing-gum wrappers. Helen promptly displayed the ingenious piece of prison art on the shelf above her desk.

Helen was completely overwhelmed when he brought her a jewelry box with a fitted lid. It was about six inches by four inches and three inches deep. Lenny had used the assorted colors of the wrappers to make a distinct pattern in the design. It was gorgeous. Lenny secreted the box into the nurse's office under his shirt and made a big show of presenting the gift.

"This is going home," Helen declared. "Thank you so much!"

"That would probably be best," Lenny responded. "You're very welcome."

Just before quitting time, a hulking monster of a man entered the examination room. This was a man who to Helen's eyes had used his yard time developing every muscle in his body to its fullest potential.

My god, his muscles have got muscles, she thought.

The man moved through the door slowly but sprinted when he saw the jewelry box on Helen's desk. Quickly sliding in her desk chair to get out of the way, Helen simultaneously reached under her desk.

"So that's what the little sneak did with it," the giant rumbled. "He promised it was for me."

The behemoth reached for Helen just as the 1,000 mg injection of propofol went into his neck. "Ack," was all he said as he hit the floor like a steer felled in a slaughterhouse.

Gathering her things, Helen pushed the call button for the guard. "He tried to attack me. I gave him something to make him sleep. He'll be up in a few minutes. You all need to put that animal in solitary."

Helen did not return to Piedmont Prison. She declined to participate in the incident follow-up at the prison but did give a deposition. Telling her side of the story was necessary to receive her disability benefits from the state. Helen's claim stated, "While I was not physically harmed in the incident, I was traumatized and find that I am unable to perform the duties required as a result of the attack."

"I just don't feel safe going back to that place," she declared to anyone who would listen. To the Golden Girls she would tell the story over and over of how lucky she had been to hit the lottery with a full retirement package after only working for a few weeks.

The preloaded syringe Velcroed under her desktop belied her inability to defend herself. Not wanting her intentions to be misinterpreted, Helen had been careful to dispose of the syringe off site. If the investigators wondered about its whereabouts, they didn't ask.

Fortunately, the size of the man saved his life. A smaller prisoner would have died on the spot. Only Helen knew whether the hidden injections came in "Small" or "Large," and she never told anyone.

CONVERSATION

"Well, you certainly made a jerk of yourself tonight."

"How do you mean?"

"You couldn't take your eyes off of Tammy all night."

"If she didn't want everybody looking at her, she shouldn't have worn that dress."

"So, you're blaming her for your wandering eyes?"

"My wandering eyes? My wandering eyes? How do you get that?"

"I get that from you walking around positioning yourself in front of Tammy all night."

"Did not."

"Did so."

"Well, how about you laughing at every word out of that jackal Frank's mouth?"

"What? Whatever are you talking about?"

"I'm talking about you laughing at Frank's tired replay of last night's *Tonight Show*. It seems like over the years that we've known them that he could come up with some original material."

"You're just jealous because he makes people laugh, and people like him."

"I don't think so. I think what you hear is people being polite, with one notable exception."

"Me? Me? You're saying that I'm the one notable exception?"

"Well, if the shoe fits."

"Don't forget to stop and get milk for the kids' breakfast tomorrow."

"I won't. I'm just going to try that new Stop and Shop. If they're well stocked, they could save us a few miles on our grocery runs."

"If their prices aren't sky-high."

"Of course."

~   ~   ~

"Well, how much was it?"

"Two seventy-five a gallon. That's about a dime more than the grocery store, but way more convenient. They look pretty well stocked too."

"Judy Elrod told me she thought she could just go into the grocery store every other week and go to the Stop and Shop in between."

"Well, Judy's just got her and her three cats. It is still just three, right?"

"How would I know? I'm not her cat wrangler. I do take your point; three cats are a lot different than three kids."

"Two of which are teenagers and eat like they think the zombie apocalypse is coming at any time."

"Well, somebody is still up unless they forgot to turn off the TV. You carry the milk. I've got the key."

"Looks like they heard us coming and ran to get into bed. You go do the bed check, and I'll lock up down here."

"You coming to bed?"

"In a little while. I'm going to watch a little of *The Tonight Show*. I want to see if I can get a preview of Frank's routine for next week."

"Well, don't be up too long. Tomorrow is going to be a big day."

"I know, I won't."

~ ~ ~

"Your snoring is waking up the neighbors."

"Is not."

"I don't know why we can't get a little TV for the bedroom like most people have so when you fall asleep, you'll already be in bed."

"Because studies show that people who fall asleep with their TVs on all night don't get a restful sleep."

"If you were any more restful, you'd have six feet of dirt covering you."

"You'd like that, wouldn't you?"

"No, I wouldn't like that. You think I want to raise these kids by myself?"

"Well, I bet you wouldn't be by yourself for long. Ol' Frank would be over here every night regaling you and the kids with the latest knock-knock jokes. He wouldn't wait for my body to get cold."

"I don't know why you keep doing that. Are you that insecure, or are you just that antisocial?"

"Do what? Call you out on your little admirer and his antics?"

"If you weren't insecure, it wouldn't bother you. You would realize that I've 'plighted my troth' to you."

"Maybe I didn't get feelings of insecurity until I saw you and Frank making goo-goo eyes at each other. Like the old saying goes, 'You're not paranoid if people really are out to get you.'"

"That's ridiculous. Goo-goo eyes? Where do you come up with these things?"

"I use my astute powers of observation. Of course, lately I don't even have to attempt to be perceptive. You guys are just right out in the open with your flirtations."

"Would you stop hogging the covers? My feet are freezing, and I need to get to sleep. We've got a big day tomorrow."

"So you keep saying, but is it really?"

"Well, most people count a twentieth anniversary as a big deal, but I'm sure you've figured out a way to throw cold water on that too."

"No, no plans. I just think it's weird, ironic—whatever the word is. We're inviting a bunch of people over to celebrate our twentieth anniversary, and one of the invitees is trying to make sure we don't make it to twenty-one."

"I think you are delusional. Will you please just shut up so I can get to sleep?"

"Sure, we can sleep, but the problem will still be there when we wake up."

"The problem is in your head, or with your head. I'm not sure which."

"Well, if it's just in my head, tell me why our youngest told me you guys stopped by 'Uncle Frank's' after soccer practice?"

"Uh, because I was telling Frank and Tammy about our anniversary plans. I wanted to reinforce to them not to do anything on our account."

"And all of the cell towers were down, and you couldn't call either one of them?"

"No, the cell towers weren't all down. Their house is on the way back from the soccer fields, and I just thought it would be nicer to stop in person rather than call."

"The old personal touch, is that it?"

"Why do you try to make something out of something that is a totally socially acceptable situation?"

"Because you took our daughter to your boyfriend's house and had her wait in the car while you conducted business."

"She was in the car for, like, five minutes."

"Not what she said. She said she had to go to the bathroom so bad that she went up and knocked on the door. She said she was about to go around back when you finally came to the door."

"Well, I think the urgency of the moment has clouded her perception of time. I was just on the other side of the door and answered it right away."

"So you say. But why didn't you mention it to me that night when I got home? Why do I need to hear about your assignations from our daughter?"

"Assignations? Did you look that up? Was it in your Word for the Day calendar? Jesus!"

"Let's not bring Him into this. There's already enough of us in this relationship."

"You have truly lost your mind!"

"Perhaps, but as insane as I might be, I know that I've always been true to you. I have always honored our vows."

"And you're implying that I haven't? You're taking our daughter's bathroom emergency to fabricate some sort of affair between me and Frank? Frank? If I was going to throw it all away, don't you think I'd aim a little higher than Frank?"

"Maybe, but what if you didn't want to throw it all away? What if you wanted to have your cake and eat it too?"

"I'm confused. Are you the cake, or is Frank? My god, you're delusional."

"Maybe, maybe. I keep telling myself I'm just being paranoid, I'm being insecure, but the feeling won't go away. After Frank's performance for one tonight, I was sure of it."

"Sure of what?"

"Sure that there is something going on with you and Frank that is much deeper than a platonic friendship."

"And what has your Spidey-sense concluded?"

"It's concluded that you're hiding something big, and that all of the clues point to you and Frank planning a future without me and the kids. Maybe you're going to run off to Bora Bora or someplace. I guess Frank's got enough money to set you all up anywhere in the world. At least he brags like he does."

"So, what if he is rich? There's nothing wrong with being successful, trying to achieve. Do you think I'd leave you and the kids for money?"

"Don't forget his witty patter. If he loses his fortune in the divorce, you'll always have his comedy routine to fall back on, on those rainy days."

"Divorce? Whose divorce? Did Tammy say something to you? Are you just baiting me to see if I'll admit to something that's not there?"

"Tammy didn't say anything to me. I think she's oblivious to what's going on. She seems more concerned with getting the perfect spray-on tan than she is with whether her husband is tomcatting around."

"OK, let's assume for a minute that I'm not having—What was your word?—an 'assignation' with Frank. Do you think that Tammy is suspicious that Frank is seeing someone else? Did she mention someone's name? I bet it's his secretary."

"No, Tammy didn't mention anyone's name. Curious that you're curious though. Is that jealousy creeping through?"

"There's nothing to be jealous of because there's nothing there."

"Then why do you seem so worried?"

"I'm worried because I think you might have a malignant tumor in your brain or something. Honest to God, do you think about this all of the time?"

"Not all of the time. Some of the time I think about what if the shoe was on the other foot and Tammy wasn't such a bubbleheaded bleached blonde. What would it be like to run off with her and Frank's money to Bora Bora."

"I'm convinced you've got a brain tumor. We're going to get you to a doctor and have your head examined."

"That's fine. I know what I know, and even if I've got a tumor squeezing my brain like an octopus crushing a clam, it doesn't change the fact that I know something is up with you and Frank."

"You are completely and absolutely delusional. Is there any chance you're going to let me sleep tonight, or are you going to continue to babble until you run out of steam?"

"Fine, go to sleep. I don't know how your conscience will let you sleep, but that's on you."

"My conscience is fine. I'm just hoping your tumor doesn't crush what's left of your brain before morning. Night."

"Night."

~   ~   ~

"Hey, wake up. There's something I've got to show you."

"Jesus, it's ten thirty. Why did you let me sleep so late?"

"Because you were doing such a good job of it. It's your superpower. Come over here, I want to show you something."

"What are Frank and Tammy doing in that sports car in our driveway at ten thirty in the morning? More importantly, why are they continuing to lay down on the horn? They're going to wake the whole neighborhood."

"That's the plan. We want everybody to see your anniversary gift. It's a 1967 Corvette split window coupe in Rally Red. Frank took it in in trade about six months ago from a guy that didn't know what it was worth. It's got about eight thousand miles on it and is in perfect condition. Knowing your obsession with cars, Frank asked if I'd be interested in a really good deal. He's selling it to us for what he's got in it, which is about a tenth of its market value. It's been really hard keeping it a secret. I thought Daphne might let the cat out of the bag when we stopped by their house to sign the paperwork."

"It's mine?"

"It's yours and Frank's finance company. Why are you crying? I thought you'd be happy."

"I am happy. I mean, I'm relieved, and I will be happy. I just have a little confession to make."

"A confession. About what?"

"I filed for a divorce this week. The process server is going to deliver the papers to you here today. I knew you'd be here."

"What? You're kidding, right? You're making a sick, twisted joke, right?"

"No, but I can take it all back. I'll make it all disappear. I'll un-file, or whatever it's called, on Monday. I was just convinced that you wanted to be with Frank. I thought our anniversary would be a fitting day to set you free and let you be happy. I'll fix it, I promise."

"No, that's OK. I'm good."

"You're good. What does that mean?"

"Just that. I'm good."

THE ACCIDENT

It was a particularly miserable, hot, humid day. The sweltering heat was compounded by the heat stored in the concrete of the interstate. It had been an unseasonably warm spring. The literal hell on earth was I-4 westbound from Orlando. The occupants encased in hundreds of cars lined up to take the exit ramp to Disney World all shared one goal: to get to the Magic Kingdom before their excitement and jubilation turned to exasperation and mayhem.

Suddenly, it looked as though the roadblock had cleared. The traffic in front of the blue Expedition carrying the young family began to move ahead at a normal clip. Bill Simmons slipped his land yacht into drive and pressed the accelerator. The usually forty-five-minute trip from their home in Kissimmee was now in its second hour. Turning quickly to his children, Todd, age eight, and Gracie, age six, Bill contorted his face as he said in his Donald Duck voice, "This is a fine kettle of fish!" As he continued his "bawahahahahaha" through his cheeks and tongue, he was interrupted by the shrill scream of his wife, Bobeth. "Look out!"

Before Bill could turn and face forward, the crunch of crashing metal coincided with the jolting stop of his car. As Bill looked forward, he saw that the pickup in front of him carrying long lengths of lead pipes wrapped with a red piece of tape had taken the worst of the blow. Through the steam rising from his radiator, Bill could see that the pipes had been driven through the back window of the older pickup, leaving glass shards everywhere. It appeared that the back of the child's car seat strapped in the middle of the pickup had diverted the pipes away from the child and toward the driver.

Expecting to be rear-ended himself, Bill checked his rearview mirrors. Seeing no impending danger, he cautiously unbuckled his seat belt. "Stay here, calm the kids, and I'll see if the car is drivable," he said as he cautiously opened his door and looked back at the miles of traffic now stuck again. *Geez what a day. And I had such high hopes.*

A cursory glance at the front of his car did not raise his spirits. The plaintive wails from the pickup truck ahead of him pulled him like a magnet to the driver's door. Blood and glass shards had escaped through the driver's open window. The driver's head hung to the side, still in contact with the lead pipes, which had continued on through the windshield. Bill's knees buckled as he absorbed the sight.

"Davey, Davey, Davey," a woman shouted from the passenger seat. As Bill peeked in the window, the woman caught sight of him and implored, "You've got to help him, please, he's all we got!"

"Yes, ma'am, I'll do what I can," Bill said as he gingerly touched the driver's neck, checking for a pulse. *Why am I calling her ma'am? She's half my age,* he wondered as he finally felt a steady beat. Bill turned, facing the woman in an attempt to pull open the door.

The woman began screaming hysterically in a higher pitch, "Oh god, Davey, you're dead. I can see your ghost. Oh god, Davey, don't leave us." The small child in the car seat had now begun to wail in harmony with its mother.

Bill wanted to run from the noise and the confusion of the whole episode. He opened the driver's door and began slipping the driver out of his seat belt. As Bill attempted to lift the man up in a fireman's carry, he could see through the blood-smeared face why the woman had gone into hysterics. Even through the blood and the flap of skin created by the pipes rushing past the right side of his face, the injured man was obviously Bill's double. A little thinner in the face maybe, but Bill was looking at his doppelgänger.

As he eased his twin onto his shoulders, Bill tried to find a good spot to offer aid to the injured man. He chose the grassy shoulder on the passenger's side of the truck. Bill was hopeful that the cab of the truck would block the sun's rays and provide some relief from the blistering sun.

God only knows how long it's going to take the EMTs to get here, he thought as he laid his burden down in the grass. The sound of a rusty door being opened drew Bill's attention to the passenger exiting the truck with her toddler in tow. The tall blond woman was dressed in a white T-shirt and shorts that were blood splattered. The child's left side was also sprinkled with blood. Both were wailing at the top of their lungs.

"Did you call 911?" Bill barked at the woman.

"Ain't got no cell phone. Davey's got one there in his pocket somewhere."

Rather than rifling through the pockets of the injured man, Bill pulled out his own cell phone and looked about for a mile marker or landmark that he could use to direct help to their area.

"911, what's your emergency?" the voice on the phone asked.

"Hey, we've got an accident here on I-4 at the 278-mile marker about a mile from the Disney exit. A man's been hit in the side of his head by some pipes he was carrying in the bed of his truck, and he's lost a lot of blood."

"Is he conscious?" the dispatcher asked.

"No, he's breathing, and he's got a pulse, but he's unconscious and not moving."

"OK, can you tell me, is the wound pulsing blood, or does it look like a slow trickle?"

"I'm going to go with a slow trickle if those are my options, but it's a large wound starting just behind the ear and going next to his eye. There's about a three-square-inch piece of skin just flapping on the side of his face."

"OK, you can use that flap of skin and just place something over it and apply pressure to the wound until the EMTs get there," the dispatcher said.

Bill turned to the woman, who was attempting to gain control of herself while comforting her small child. She was whimpering softly as she leaned against the open door of the truck and bounced her child on her hip.

"Do you have a clean diaper or something?" Bill asked.

"Just a disposable. Will that work? Caleb's four, and he should be potty-trained, and he mostly is, but on long days, we just put diapers on him and figure good enough."

The woman reached back into the truck and pulled out a disposable diaper. Bill took the diaper and placed the soft side against the flap of skin that he had put back in place. Now the resemblance between the men was unmistakable—very eerie.

"Do you have some wipes or something so I can clean the blood and glass off of his face?" Bill asked.

The woman reached into the truck again and then handed a box of wipes to Bill. "You might want to save some of them in case Caleb has an accident. They're pretty expensive, you know."

Bill let the caution escape into the ether. He couldn't make congruent the thought of cleaning the blood from the father of your child with being frugal about the wipes. He concentrated on the cleanup until the voice of his wife interrupted his process.

"Oh my god, it's your twin, Bill. He looks just like you. Oh my god!"

Bill looked over his shoulder. His wife and two children were looking at a scene that had to be as surreal for them as it was for him. Little Todd started crying and clutched his mother's leg for support. Gracie's lower lip stuck out, but she held it together. Bobeth was not doing quite as well as her daughter.

"Oh my god, Bill, if I didn't see both of you together, I would have thought it was you. I mean, except the clothes. You'd be wearing different clothes, and I'd wonder how you'd done that. Also, he's a little skinnier than you, but it's definitely you. Who are you all?"

The last question was aimed at the woman who was keeping track of the number of wipes being used to clean her husband.

"I'm Ada, and this here is Caleb," she said, indicating the bouncing little boy on her hip. "And that's my husband, Davey. We're the Banks." As a point of emphasis, she closed the truck door and pointed to the sign painted on the door: "Banks Plumbing." "Who the hell are you?"

"We're the Simmons. I'm Bobeth, this is Todd and Gracie, and that's my husband, Bill." Bobeth seemed about to extend her hand but must have decided against it. "How can we help? We've got cold water and juice boxes in the cooler. We've got snacks. Would you like anything? Would your little boy?"

As Ada began to answer, the howl of an ambulance siren filled the air. The sound seemed to be coming from the wrong direction, from Disney World, not Orlando. In two minutes, Bill's suspicions were confirmed when the ambulance approached, going the wrong way on the shoulder toward them. The strobing sound seemed to awaken something in the unconscious man. He opened his eyes, and the shock of seeing himself staring back at him registered on his face.

"What? What the hell? Am I dead? What's going on?" Davey began to rise up on his elbows, attempting to sit up. The injured man located his wife and child standing beside the truck. He craned his neck around to survey the rest of the scene before the two EMTs rushing in blocked his vision from his twin.

Bill relinquished his position to the medical personnel and backed away to stand next to his wife and children. He could hear some of the conversation between the three men, and Davey seemed to know who he was and more or less where he was. The EMTs placed the victim on a backboard, stabilized his neck, and began carrying him to the ambulance. Ada and the baby fell in step with the EMTs.

Bill raced to catch up. "Where are you all taking him? Can I come along?"

"Nope, sorry. We're actually not supposed to take the kid. As a matter of fact, can you bring your nephew for us? We're going to the clinic at the Magic Kingdom. The blood on your shirt will get you in," the EMT said as he grinned and slid the backboard onto the gurney and pushed the gurney into the ambulance.

"My nephew? No, I don't know these people. We just met." Bill noted the surprise in the EMT's eyes. "Seriously, we just met."

"By accident," the EMT said.

"By accident," Bill replied.

"Well, I don't know what to tell you then," the EMT said as he climbed into the ambulance. "It looks like you've got some explaining to do anyway."

Bill turned in the direction of the EMT's nod, where a Florida Highway Patrol car had just pulled up behind the stricken vehicles. He heard the ambulance's siren roar as he walked back to the wreck and the bumblebee-colored patrol vehicle.

The day started so well, he thought.

~   ~   ~

At the urging of his lawyer brother-in-law, Bill didn't try to contact Davey immediately after the accident. Florida was a no-fault insurance state, which meant that each party's insurance was responsible for fixing their insured's vehicle. Bill had not been charged in the accident. The mandated "following too close for conditions" charge had been ameliorated by the 104-degree heat, the pickup's condition, the lack of signage warning of a dangerous load, the two young children's crying about not getting to see Mickey, and possibly the knowledge that both vehicles would have to be towed and both owners faced out-of-pocket expenses. Whatever the reason, the trooper had not assigned fault to Bill, and that was a good thing according to his brother-in-law lawyer.

A month after the accident, Bill still couldn't get his twin out of his mind. He was an only child and his parents had passed away in just the last year. Both were victims of the COVID virus. First his mom had succumbed and, five days later, his dad. There was no one Bill could ask about his heritage. No one except Davey. After losing a lot of sleep and seeing his twin in every dream, Bill confronted his brother-in-law.

"I don't care what you think, I've got to talk to my twin. You can be there if you insist, but you can't talk. You can't manage the meeting. You can just be there. Got me?"

"Got you," the attorney confirmed.

The meeting was set for breakfast at the Shoney's in Kissimmee. When Davey arrived, Bill and his attorney had already secured the corner booth, and three cups of coffee had been poured. As Davey slid into the booth, the attorney let out an expletive that he then promptly repeated.

"This silver-tongued devil is my brother-in-law, Rick, and fair warning, he's also a lawyer," Bill said as he scanned the side of Davey's head while the two men shook hands. "If I didn't know you'd been in an accident, I don't think I could see where you got hit."

Davey touched the spot on the side of his head gingerly. "Yeah, the doctors at Disney World are first rate, and once my hair grew out a little bit, you can hardly see the scar."

Rick cleared his throat and said, "I know I'm not supposed to talk, but let me say, if I wasn't seeing it, I wouldn't be believing it. You too are identical. I mean, Bill's got a few pounds on you—he never met an exercise that he liked—and you're clearly getting more sunshine, but otherwise it's like looking at a reverse image. OK, I'm done. You two go ahead."

Bill began. "This is awkward. This whole thing is so unsettling, impossible, but would you be willing to get a DNA test?"

"Don't need to," Davey responded. "We're identical twins, born January 11, 1993, in Orlando Regional Medical Center to Willow Allred. Momma escaped from the Deseret Ranch and thought she had made it away clean. There was one little complication. One of the elders had left her with a special delivery that was going to arrive in about nine months."

He paused to sip his coffee. "Momma would like to meet you if you're interested. She's kinda embarrassed about giving you away, but she had her reasons."

Bill felt like ice-cold water had been thrown in his face. The shouted short orders, the clanking of dishes as the tables were being bussed only added to his delirium.

"Did you know about me?" he asked.

"Not until the night of the accident," Davey answered. "It's hard to pick between traumas from that day. Meeting a twin brother that I didn't know about won out over a near death. The truck impoundment was just icing on the cake. I confronted Momma that night."

"Geez, I'm sorry, I . . ." Bill was interrupted by his brother-in-law clearing his throat loudly. "I was just going to say that I'm sorry that my or *our* birth mother—What did you say her name was? Willow—had such a hard time of it."

"You and me both," Davey answered. "Teenage single mom is nearly impossible. Add twins to it, and I figure she started looking for a way to lighten the load. Looks like she lightened the load by about two hundred pounds." Davey grinned to show there was no malice meant in his remark.

"But how?" Bill asked. "Did she just leave me at the fire station? How did we come to be separated?"

"I asked the same question," Davey responded. "Folks back then paid a pretty penny for a healthy white baby. She figured people willing to pony up a lot of cash would be able to give you everything you wanted. It looks like she was right."

Davey paused to refill his coffee from the little pot left on the table. "You're probably going to like the answer to how she chose between us even less than I did. You were born with more hair than me. I'm older, but you had more hair. Imagine that. Mom equated that hair to you being more developed, better able to take care of yourself. Once the choice was made, Momma was able to convince herself that she had made the right decision."

Bill cut his eyes to his attorney and, catching his attention, telepathically sent the message, *We've got to check this out.* He turned back to his brother. "So, did your mom marry? Where did you grow up? Do you have any other brothers and sisters? Where do you live now?"

Davey took a breath, gathering enough wind to respond to all the questions. "Mom married a lot. Five or six times that I know about. We bounced around Apopka, Windemere, Zellwood, and Mount Dora. We went to Texas once for about a year, but that didn't work out. We came back, and Mom married Luther. He seemed to fit whatever it was she was looking for. He taught me the plumbing trade, and if it wasn't for him, I never would have got my GED or my plumber's license. What about you? Similar experience I bet." Davey gave a big grin, indicating he knew their paths had been very different.

"Well," Bill began, "Mom and Dad did give me a wonderful life just like your mom predicted. I grew up in Kissimmee, same house the whole time, graduated high school and got my engineering degree at the University of Florida. When I came out of school, I went to work with Dad developing low-cost housing. We've done pretty well, and Dad was planning on retiring this year, but he and Mom died from COVID. So now it's just me."

"Wow," Davey exhaled with feeling. "So I missed winning the lottery by a hair, or I guess a few hairs. I'd say 'Life's funny,' but it ain't really. We're scratching for every nickel and dime we can scrape together, and you're living the life of the rich and famous. One silly decision by a scared teenager that will have consequences for generations."

"That's true," Bill replied. "You've had a month to digest this, and I'm just kind of processing on the fly. It's obvious we've both got deep feelings. I'm wondering why my birth mother would reject me, and it seems like you're wishing you'd been the one rejected. There's some irony or something in there, but we can sort that out another time."

Bill turned to his lawyer and then back again to his twin. "I'd like for us to get to know each other better. I think I'd like to meet my birth mother, but I want to think about it a little more before I commit. I can help you in business. I've got a new development in St. Cloud that I haven't committed to a plumber yet. We can give you a start there and see how it goes. I'd like our accidental meeting to be serendipitous for both of us." Davey's confused look demanded that Bill clarify. "I'd like for our accident to turn out to be a good thing. Sound good?"

"I ain't looking for no handouts. I'll work hard and fair," Davey said. "But I am more aware than most that one little simple thing can put someone on a better path, so I accept your offer."

As the two men rose to shake hands, Bill grinned and said, "There will be an extensive background check, you know?"

For the first time since being separated in their infancy, the brothers wrapped their arms around each other.

COMMONALITY

The gentle rain did nothing to diminish the crowd's enthusiasm. Dozens of people protested outside the nondescript building. Some used bullhorns to amplify their message, while others yelled to the capacity of their lungs. People of all ages milled about the entrance to the building, shouting and threatening anyone who dared to approach the front door. Children as young as six years old had been incorporated into the melee. They carried signs scaled down to the strength of their bodies, but the message they carried was just as strong as the adults'.

The well-dressed woman wound her way through the slobbering cluster of acolytes, her scarf pulled tightly around her face; she hoped not to be recognized by the people clamoring about. Just the week before, she had been one of them, protesting as vociferously as the best of them. She had nearly reached the safety perimeter of the two police officers guarding the steps to the door when she heard her name called from somewhere behind her.

"Sue? Sue, is that you?"

Rather than confirm or deny her identity and be pressed to make up a wild story as to why she was going into the clinic, the woman pressed through the crowd to the double glass doors. The building's front doors had been fortified by diamond plate sheet metal to repel the inevitable stones thrown at the glass. It looked like a fortress.

"I have an appointment," she offered to the large Black man standing at the door wearing a vest with the word "SECURITY" emblazoned on the front. Neither he nor the police officers acknowledged or seemed to notice her passing. The crowd roared its disapproval as she opened the door and slid inside.

Just inside stood a formidable metal desk whose occupant had a direct sight line to the door. The receptionist's eyes flicked between the woman, the clipboard holding that day's appointments, and the crowd outside.

"Sue Patton. I have an appointment at ten thirty," the woman said.

"Got it." The receptionist handed the woman a clipboard with questionnaires to be completed. "Walk through the metal detector, find a seat, fill these out, and hand them to the nurse when they call your name."

"I have a gun. Do I leave it with you?" the woman asked.

"Why in the . . . Never mind." The receptionist pushed a button under the desk, and the security guard posted at the front door turned around. When the receptionist made a *Come here* motion with her finger, the guard entered the building.

"This lady would like for you to hold something for her until she leaves." The receptionist gestured for the woman to hand the pistol to the security guard.

"Nice," the guard commented as he unchambered the round from the Glock and removed the magazine. He placed the weapon inside his vest.

"Anything else?" he asked the room. Responses in the negative freed him to return to his post at the door.

Once inside the waiting room, the woman was confronted with a room full of patients and significant others and not enough chairs. A young waif of a girl caught Sue's eye and moved the raincoat and umbrella from the seat beside her.

"Thanks," said Sue as she arranged herself in the seat.

The young girl started speaking while she was still bent over stowing her items under her chair. "I thought he was gonna come, and I was saving him a seat, but he musta got caught in traffic or something. With all this rain, the traffic has to be real bad."

"Ah yeah, I guess so," Sue said. "It's pretty nasty outside."

"Yeah, that too. Kenneth don't like confrontations. He mighta seen that crowd and decided not to fight against 'em. I'm Anna, by the way," the girl said as she reached out her hand.

"Sue," the woman said as she extended her hand. "Have you been waiting long?"

"Seems like forever," the girl replied. "Ain't it funny how a thing you want to put off forever can't come quick enough once you've decided to do it? Of course, I'm just speaking for myself. As Kenneth says, 'We've got all the time in the world to start a family,' and I guess we do. It's just right now with Kenneth in college and me in high school, a baby ain't gonna help either one of us realize our full potential. That's how Kenneth says it—'realizing our full potential.'"

The girl paused, maybe expecting a share from Sue, or perhaps she had lost her train of thought. Sue bore down on the questionnaires, pretending that the queries were so difficult she needed to focus all her resources on them. Sue didn't want to share or even engage. She didn't want to tell the girl that she was a cliché. Just another dewy-eyed high school girl seduced by a college "man." She didn't want to tell Anna that her beau was probably in a bar somewhere waiting for Anna's call. A call that would free him from his responsibility and probably from Anna. Besides, Sue sharing her story required telling the high school girl the circumstances by which they had been thrown into the same lifeboat.

Sue deliberated slowly on the documents. Part of her lack of haste in completing the medical survey was the uncontrollable self-reflection of her situation. Her brain continued to confront her with the facts that led to how she, too, was in the same boat as the young girl.

Nearing the end of her fecundity, Sue had convinced herself she was no longer capable of bearing children. But multiple tests from the drugstore foretold a potential social disaster. Sue chose to seek absolute confirmation from the clinic. Her personal doctor was an elder in their church and would never have been able to keep the secret. The exam was scheduled at a time when Sue knew her church group would not be out front. To her horror, the exam confirmed Sue's worst suspicions.

Getting the appointment for the procedure had not been as easy as the exam. Sue's church group knew which days of the month the doctors came into town to perform the procedures. There was no way to make it into the building for the appointment other than running the gauntlet of The Full Gospel Original Church of God. Sue was hopeful that her disguise had been deceptive enough to deny any allegations that "so and so had seen Sue with their own two eyes."

Having procrastinated with the paperwork as long as she could, Sue slipped the pen under the clip of the clipboard and looked about the room. It was truly a cross section of the community. Probably 95 percent female, but these were women of all ages and walks of life. *Add a preacher's wife to the census,* Sue thought as she turned her attention to the girl next to her. "How old are you, sweetie, if you don't mind me asking?"

"Sixteen. Seventeen next month," Anna answered.

"And how old is your boyfriend? Kenneth, did you say?" Sue asked.

"He'll be twenty-one next month. Our birthdays are one day apart."

One day and four years apart, which in this state could bring a statutory rape charge, Sue thought. *I bet there's a young man somewhere sweating bullets right now.*

Taking Sue's silence for disapproval, Anna responded quickly, "We could get married. In fact, we don't even need to get married. It's just that the timing's not right for us to start a family right now."

"You won't be able to reach your full potential," Sue said. "Yeah, I get it. I agree."

It was about this point that Sue would normally start asking questions of the unwed expectant mother about the unborn child and how it was going to reach its full potential. But not today. No, today, Sue would not be allowed to cast any stones. Today, Sue stood before God and Anna and everyone as who she truly was—a sinner. She was a sinner, an adulterer, and a fornicator, and God had sent her here to this place without shame to be humbled.

"Number twelve," the nurse called from the door to the procedure rooms.

"Won't be long now," Anna said as she held up her clipboard to Sue, revealing the *14* in the corner.

Anna and Sue watched the Black woman gather her things and head toward the nurse. The clipboard containing her personal information was her key to the rooms beyond, and she was allowed entrance. Surprisingly, the door made a very audible locking sound as it shut.

Anna began to fidget in her chair. "I wish Kenneth had come. I know I'm doing the right thing. I just wish he was here."

"You're doing the right thing, honey, believe me," Sue said as she surveyed the other women in the room and tried to imagine their circumstances. The poor were easy to pick out. Many had arrived without umbrellas or raincoats and were drip-drying as they awaited their turn. The naive schoolgirls were revealed by their youth. Some sat with friends, others with a parent or guardian. Only one sat with who Sue presumed was a boyfriend. Only one white woman appeared to be in her late twenties or early thirties. Sue was the sole representative of her age group.

Reflecting on the circumstances of others helped Sue to keep her mind off her situation, but it wasn't long before Sue came back to her predicament.

"Number thirteen," the nurse called from the door. The redheaded girl sitting with her blond friend gathered up her belongings and headed toward the nurse. "Text me when you're done," her friend called out, grabbing her own things. Sue assumed the friend would wait in the parking lot until called.

The patients generally left via a side door. The patient discharge area was controlled by a chain-link fence and a guard to keep the protesters at bay. Sue would be discharged to an Uber driver who would be responsible for returning her to her car in the lot. *If there's a just God, none of my friends will be leaving at the same time I am*, she thought.

Anna was fidgeting with her paperwork, and Sue could feel the tension rising in the teenager. "Have you got somebody at home that'll be watching you during your recovery?" Sue asked.

"Momma and Daddy will be there if something goes wrong. I guess I'll have to tell them if something goes wrong, but I don't think it will," Anna replied. "I'll be OK. Have you got somebody waiting for you?"

"No, I came on my own, but I've got a plan," Sue answered. "Do you have a backup plan since your boyfriend didn't make it? Do you need a ride? Do you have money for an Uber?"

Anna's eyes began to spin like slot-machine reels. Her face gave the appearance of one who had just realized that she not only didn't have a ride but lacked the funds to call one. "I've got about ten dollars. I guess I'll go as far as that will get me. I'm strong. I can walk the rest. Maybe Kenneth will have made it through the traffic jam and can pick me up when I'm through."

Sue reached into her purse and handed the girl a twenty-dollar bill. She wanted to tell the girl to never count on Kenneth again for anything except heartache, but she resisted the urge.

"I can pay you back," Anna said. "In fact, I might not even need it. Kenneth might still come. Tell me your name and address, and I'll be sure to get it to you."

"No, dear, that's all right," Sue replied. "Us girls have to stick together. I was just about your age when I met a man that I was sure was sent to me by God. He was a seminary student and was about the most handsome rascal I'd ever seen."

"What happened?" Anna asked.

"Well, we got married, he became a preacher, and I became a preacher's wife. It's been a good life, I guess."

Sue did not divulge that her husband's preference in women had not aged as they had. Sarcastically she thought, *And you, my little partner in sin, are already past his sell-by date.* Instead, she said, "But I often think about what might have happened if I had stayed in school. Recognized my full potential." Sue smiled at the girl. "Who knows, I might have been an astronaut, or an author. Alas, that ship has sailed."

"I know this is personal, and you don't have to answer, but why are you here?" Anna asked.

"I'm here because I'm a woman, and I want to be loved." Sue bit her lip as she bridged the generational gap. "I want to be the most important person in somebody's life. I want someone to smile at me every time they see me. I want someone to care how *my* day has been. I want someone to recognize my sacrifice and struggle, and I want to be their 'one and only.'"

A single tear slid down Sue's cheek, and Anna looked away while Sue dabbed at it with a tissue.

"But I'm sure your kids love you. I'm sure you're their 'one and only,'" Anna offered.

"No, no kids. We tried. I thought the same thing. I'll have a houseful of kids, and they'll love me, and we'll be happy no matter what." Sue sighed. "But it was not to be. God chose to make my husband fruitful in other ways, I guess."

Before Anna could comment on the revelation, the nurse at the door called, "Number fourteen."

"That's me. Seriously, if you tell me your name, I'll get your money back to you," Anna said as she gathered her things.

"No, your money is worthless to me, but I do want you to think about what you are worth." Sue looked deeply into the young girl's eyes. "Don't sell yourself short. Don't give yourself to someone who is not worthy of the gift. Use this experience to inform you in your future decisions, and never settle for someone that doesn't put you first come hell or high water, or a little bit of rain."

The awkward silence at the end of the soliloquy was broken by the nurse repeating, "Number fourteen."

Anna rushed through the door, and it locked loudly behind her.

Sue was left alone with her thoughts but not for long. Anna's seat was immediately taken by a Hispanic girl that didn't seem to have Anna's propensity to share. Sue reached inside her purse for a mint. She offered one to the girl, but the girl declined with a "No, gracias." Sue decided not to try out her "missionary Spanish." Caring about others had already cost her twenty dollars; maybe now was the time to just wait until her number was called.

The mint brought back memories of her first encounter with the youth pastor. Of all the things to consider in beginning a relationship with a man twenty years her junior, the one thing Sue had become obsessed about was her breath. *Dim lighting and covers can obscure a lot of flaws, but not your breath,* Sue thought at the time.

As she sucked on the mint, her mind wandered. Sue would never be quite sure of the young man's intentions, or his motivations. Whatever his motive had been for seeking a relationship with a much older woman who was also his boss's wife, he had thrown himself into the affair with a youthful gusto. That vigorous enthusiasm reminded Sue of happier days when she had felt needed. When the two red lines appeared on the pregnancy test, Sue knew the affair was over. There was foolishness, there was wicked sinfulness, and she was guilty of both. Sue would not allow her shame to be cast on another.

"Number twenty-one," the nurse called from the door. Sue double-checked her clipboard and gathered her things. The nurse smiled and reached for the clipboard as Sue walked through the door leading to the examination rooms.

"We're in number three, here, on the left," the nurse said as she opened the door for Sue.

Inside the examination room, the nurse reviewed the questionnaires. "Everything seems to be in order. Just remove your clothes and put on this gown. You can hang your clothes there. The doctor will be with you in just a minute."

As Sue began to undress, it occurred to her how fortuitous it was that the legislative bill her church was instrumental in sponsoring had failed. The bill requiring the father's permission to terminate a pregnancy had failed by one vote. One vote had saved Sue, her husband, the youth minister, and truly her entire church public ridicule and shame. One vote. Had it not been for that one vote, Sue's life would have been turned upside down. Sue felt a pang of guilt for the scorn her church had heaped on the legislator when they outed him. *I didn't know then what I know now*, Sue thought as she lay back on the table and waited for the doctor.

The procedure was quick and painless, and before she knew it, Sue was in a recovery room with a group of women. All were waiting for the required time before they were released. Sue looked about her and wondered whether they would acknowledge each other if they saw one another out in public. She was quite certain she would purposefully not recognize anyone from today. She was hopeful the rest of the patients felt the same way. What a horrible way to end the question, "Where do I know you from?"

Sue's hour was up, and she dressed and called for an Uber. She felt good physically but listened intently to the nurse's instructions of what to do should things turn sour. Sue realized she was still feeling the effects of the mild sedative they had given her. She didn't want to engage in activity that might cause any scrutiny of any physical symptoms she might develop because of her imprudence.

From the back porch of the center Sue could see the Uber being waved through the gates. The area was completely protected from public view, but Sue covered her head and face tightly with her scarf. As she stepped down the steps to the waiting car a voice called from behind her, "Wait, wait." Sue turned to see the security guard from the front door holding out her pistol and its magazine. "I had to wait until you were out of the secure area. You understand."

"I do, thank you," Sue gave a wry grin. "Never leave home without it," she said as she slipped the gun in her purse.

"Where to?" the very dark Black man asked as Sue stepped into the car.

Sue reached forward with a twenty-dollar bill as she said, "The parking lot on the other side of Gallieon Park. I know it's a short trip. That's why I'm giving you such a big tip. I'm going to sit very low in the seat, so please don't talk to me or give the impression that you've got a fare."

"Yes, ma'am." The driver engaged the gears, and in a few minutes was parking his car in the parking lot next to the only other car parked there.

Sue got out and watched the driver leave before opening her trunk and swapping out her tan raincoat for a navy blue one. Her tan scarf was replaced by a multicolored kaleidoscope-patterned one. Her black pumps were exchanged for white tennis shoes, and the black umbrella was replaced by a clear plastic one with dark blue raindrops splashing across the expanse.

Satisfied that she had done as well as she could to change her identity, Sue started her car and headed for the parking lot that adjoined the center. She parked her car in the only available spot and took a second to compose herself. Looking in the car's makeup mirror for signs in her face that might reveal where she had been that day, she found none. Sue declared herself "ready for action." She walked directly to her oldest and dearest friend, Angie, who was shouting into a bullhorn. Sue waited patiently for Angie to pause and catch her breath before speaking.

"What did I miss?" she inquired.

DREAMS

The aspiring author read the online instructions for submissions one last time before pressing Enter on his keyboard:

"To be considered for publication, paste your query letter in the form below. In order for Tontitown Premier Press to give your work a fair evaluation, please include the first five pages of your work in the block provided. If interested, we will request to see more. Please allow up to 8 weeks for our response before inquiring. Your query letter must include your Full Name, Email, Phone, Title, Genre, Word Count, Synopsis, and Agent Email, if applicable. Please include previously published works even if they were self-published."

He reread his query letter for the hundredth time and ran spell-check on it one last time. It was his seventh submission for the day, and he prayed that seven would be his lucky number. Of course, he had done an invocation with each of his submissions. *You're the one. It takes two. Third time's the charm.* And so on. Averaging seven submissions a day for one week would get the writer through the fifty publishing houses he had identified that were looking for "new exciting authors" in his genre.

He wasn't sure whether his odds were one in fifty based off his submissions or whether they were closer to one in a million. He hoped that his choice of publishers in the genre of Christian drama would be narrow enough to give his work a chance. Most of the publishers of general fiction were closed to submissions. The Big Five publishers took submissions only by referral, either from an agent, which Adam couldn't afford, or some other insider with connections within the industry. Adam wasn't connected, but he had hopes and dreams of changing all that.

As Adam hit the Send button he wondered how or why the Big Five were always referred to as "the Big Five." He was always reading about this or that publisher merging with another or going out of business. He doubted that the current Big Five were the same Big Five from a decade ago. The idea that numbers six and seven were biting their nails, waiting in the wings for their chance to attain Big Five status amused him.

Shutting down his word processor for the day, he was reminded once again by his title page that he was not Adam Samuels but Addison Starke. He had picked Addison not only for its nonbinary usage but also because the name Addison's Old English meaning was "son of Adam." That "son of himself" was the persona he hoped to develop. A new Adam that would be able to reach people through his words. Addison would shape minds, be an influencer. He just needed the right publisher to bring his works to market. The agent and public relations person would soon follow; he was sure of it.

As Adam rifled back and forth through his spine-broken copy of *Writer's Market*, purchased used from Amazon at a deep discount, he wondered if perhaps the information contained within was the problem. He had received a few "rejections" by way of bad email addresses, which he presumed to mean that the company was no longer in business. He considered buying a more recent copy as he washed his hands and prepared to eat dinner.

"Looks good, honey," he said, sitting down to a plate piled high with spaghetti and meat sauce.

"Well, I hope you like it. I'm working evening shift the rest of the week, so you're going to have to fend for yourself after tonight," replied his wife, Sarah, as she brought the bread to the table. "How's the writing business coming?" She sprayed parmesan cheese over the top of her spaghetti.

"It's going, it's going," Adam replied, and took the cheese from his wife. "I sent out seven more submissions today. What's that old saying? 'Throw enough stuff at the wall and some of it's bound to stick,' right?"

"Now, don't be too hard on yourself," Sarah said. "I like your book, and I bet a lot of other people will find it inspirational too. It hasn't been easy for you to tell people about your childhood and open up all those old wounds. Besides, now that you're retired, you can spend your day doing whatever you want to do. That's as long as you don't take up some expensive hobby like woodworking or ballroom dancing."

"Yeah, even with you still working I don't think there's enough money available for me to learn how to rumba. Although I do think you'd look good in one of those long slinky dresses," Adam joked while giving his wife a salacious wink.

They spent the rest of the meal eating quickly and silently. Completely full, Adam got up from the table, rinsed his plate in the sink, and placed it in the dishwasher.

"Hopefully this writing thing will take off and you can retire early, and we'll be able to take dance lessons or a cruise. Maybe buy an RV, you just never know."

"I hope so, honey, if just for your sake," Sarah said, placing her plate in the dishwasher next to Adam's. "It seems like you're working almost as hard every day as you used to even though the book is finished, am I right?"

"Well, not as hard, and it's certainly not as painful as dredging up all of those old memories. But it's pretty frustrating trying to crack the door open at a publishing house." Adam flopped into his giant Barcalounger and reached for the remote. "That old adage about knowing somebody sure appears to be true in the book business. I'm tempted to self-publish, but from what I've read none of the agents or anyone in the publishing world will ever take you seriously if you self-publish. It's like the title of the book is supposed to burn a hole in an editor's or intake person's brain." Adam began to flip through the channels rapidly, looking for their usual Monday night programming.

"Well, I'm sure you'll figure it out," Sarah said, and patted his shoulder. "You always do."

~ ~ ~

The email from Tontitown Premier Press came as a shock. As Adam read it over and over, he tingled with excitement. From the signature it appeared he had caught the interest of someone high up in the organization.

Hi Adam,

Your query for *Nobody Here but Us Chickens* interests us, and we would like to see more. Please send the full manuscript as a Word document, and we will get back to you as soon as possible.

Warm Regards,

Annie Carson

Deputy Publisher — Faith imprint

Senior Editor

Media Liaison

TONTITOWN PREMIER PRESS

The email was his first and, so far, only positive response. He quickly discarded the notion of not responding immediately for fear of looking eager. Adam attached the full manuscript in a return email with his warmest regards to Annie Carson. He drew a big *X* on the wall calendar hanging above his desk. To clarify the notation, he wrote *Sent to TPP* in red letters on that day's date, January 21. Sitting back down at his desk, he smiled to himself. He envisioned the calendar filled with *X*s and red-lettered notations.

He couldn't wait to tell Sarah the news. Normally, she would wake up about noon, and they would have lunch together. They usually visited for a few hours before she had to get ready for the evening shift. Adam was aware Sarah was having to deal with not only the strain of working the evening shift but also being his biggest booster. The lack of positive responses in his email had started to wear him down a bit. *Today is just the beginning,* he told himself as he jubilantly climbed the steps from his basement office to the main floor.

When he received the follow-up email from TPP on April 24, TPP was still the only *X* marked on the calendar. In spite of it being three months since his last communication, the email gave an instant boost to his spirits. The responses to his other submissions for the most part had been kind but no less discouraging. All the carefully crafted, beautifully constructed words contained in the forty or so responses he had received could be encapsulated in two letters: *N-O.* The email from TPP was quite the opposite. Adam zoomed in on the email so that its words took up the whole screen. It read:

Hi Adam,

Thank you for sending *Nobody Here but Us Chickens* for consideration. We would like for you to resubmit when the comments below have been addressed.

Thank you,

Annie Carson

Analysis

2–3 paragraph analysis: strengths and weaknesses?

I enjoyed the narrative structure of the entries because it gives the story a fun, unique voice, and I was intrigued. Bud's world and his current struggles are set up right at the beginning too, which made me root for him. There are a lot of funny moments in this manuscript! (A favorite of mine being, "Well, as my dear departed daddy, Bocephus Lyte, used to say, 'I'm as tired as a fly in a nudist colony.'"—Too funny!) Your story would be better served by giving the characters something to do and letting the reader surmise who they are based on how they handle the situation. In chapter 6, you mention that your main character wants to apologize to his family for what he's done. I was intrigued, but then you go back to talking about family members and what they've done. This may be an opportunity to tell readers about some more funny/terrible things that the character did. I really like your main character (I'm rooting for him!) and I want to read more about the things that he does. Please give us a revised manuscript when you have addressed these issues.

Adam started on the revisions immediately. He had Sarah proofread them that night. Before resubmitting the revised manuscript to the publisher, he reached out to his brother Jacob and had him read the entire manuscript once again. Adam reasoned that because it was a story about *their* family, Jacob should bear some of the burden of catching typos and inaccuracies. Asking his brother for favors could be a tricky thing, and Adam feared the prospect of his brother asking for a co-author title. To his surprise, Jacob returned his revised version in just a couple of weeks, no strings attached. Adam began his revision of Jacob's revision and proudly passed the completed work back to the publisher on May 13.

Encouraged by the fact that a publisher, even if it was just one, was interested in his words, Adam began working furiously on a second novel. He was hopeful that he had found a niche, and so he set the second book in the same location and utilized a few of the same characters from his first book. The recurring characters were used in tangential ways to the main plot of the second book. Adam felt that he was quite clever in placing his characters in different settings in the two books, showing the different aspects of their lives. On June 1, Adam received an email from the publisher that read in part:

Hi Adam,

We have finished reviewing *Nobody Here but Us Chickens*. I wanted to share our focus group's reader comments with you, as well as comments from one of our editors. Here is what they had to say. We look forward to a resubmission.

Analysis:

The transition into chapter 6 was well done and a welcome dive into some details that actually let me get to know Bud. The flow of character descriptions and the buildup of Bud's life story from these descriptions was great; I felt really invested. The story is an amazing balance of a good man's endeavor to do right by someone who has hurt him.

The buildup through a brief family history in the first few chapters was absolutely necessary to my enjoyment of the rest of it. The epilogue was a fantastic little touch, and it helped resolve everything and make it feel like the story had a very real connection to the present.

From the description of the book, I was worried that this story would be a demonization of the women in one man's life, but I was happily surprised by the realism, believable drama, and healthy rationality and personal practices that Bud was able to execute. It made him a character that I hoped the best for in life.

I like this book, but I would recommend an editing and a resubmission. There is a lot of repetition, and it really needs to be edited for urgency so that every word counts. I found myself skimming instead of reading, and that's a telltale sign that it needs a good editing session.

Adam didn't know what to think. He thought he had done everything asked of him, and clearly some of the readers liked the book. He was so consumed with his second book that it was hard for him to return to the first. The characters in the first book were drawn from Adam's life. If the characters were not appealing to the readers, didn't that say something? Wasn't that the story?

Could he, for what felt like the one hundredth time, make changes to the story of his life to make it more appealing to the readers? Mean characters repeated bad behavior. How does that not become repetitive when you're covering the expanse of one's life? It is the repetition of that behavior in a lifelong relationship that is soul crushing, that leaves people broken and without hope.

He shared the email with Sarah for her input over lunch.

"Well, they seem to like it," Sarah said positively. "Maybe it's the layout of the book. Maybe the choices you made in how you're telling the story are throwing the readers off."

"I don't know," Adam said through bites of last night's pizza. "It's the book I had to write to maintain my sanity, and people seem to be amused. It just seems like they're being picky about stuff that I thought editors were supposed to clean up for you."

"What's an editor supposed to do?" Sarah said as she sipped on her iced tea.

"All of the stuff they're talking about as near as I can tell," Adam answered. "I did see on the internet where TPP's editors also have their own editing companies. I can't imagine having to do as much reading as they have to do for their job and still having the time or the energy to take on other jobs."

"You don't think that's what they're trying to do, do you?" Sarah asked as she got up from the table. "You don't think they're trying to scare up business for their side gigs, do you?"

"I don't know," Adam answered. "They look legitimate from everything I've seen, but I guess that doesn't mean that much in this time of online businesses. They could be in China for all I know, but their address is in Arkansas."

"Well, it's your thing," she said, and laid an arm across Adam's shoulders. "Just be sure that if you're going to do it, it's going to make you happy. It doesn't have to make any money or make you famous, but it can't make you sad. These are your happy years. This is when you get to do all of the silly stuff you couldn't do while you were working. And, no, I'm not saying your writing is silly. I'm saying if you want to chase a golf ball or learn to crochet, I don't care, as long as you're happy doing it. If what you're doing makes you sad, you need to quit doing it. Life's just too darn short."

"You're right, and I'm not sad. I'll just call it amused until I get a better word. I'm just excited about the new book, and it feels like there's some feet dragging going on at the publishers. Mentally, I'd like to say *Chickens* is done and move on to number two."

"Well, I guess you can't count your chickens quite yet," Sarah said as she gave her husband of forty years a wink.

"How long have you been waiting to share that one?" Adam asked.

Sarah chuckled. "Not long."

~ ~ ~

Adam worked furiously on his rewrite and was overjoyed to receive a publishing contract on July 1. He ran up the steps from his basement office at a pace he had not attempted in the last twenty years to share the news with Sarah. She seemed to be as excited for him as he was.

I'm going to be an author. Not just a writer. A real, honest-to-God author, he thought as he drifted off to sleep that night.

Adam's business mind tempered his writer's enthusiasm the following day as he absorbed the fifteen pages of legalese that constituted the publishing contract. Trying to maintain his excitement through what was as one-sided an agreement as he had ever seen, he rationalized with himself over almost every clause. Exclusive rights to all media forms including movies, audible, and CDs were relinquished. Royalties were so small as to be nonexistent, and the contract was for three years from the book's publication date, not the contract date. The publisher's obligations were minimal and, with regard to promotion, almost nonexistent. *What does 'promote on our social media outlets' mean?* Adam thought while he put pen to paper and signed away his rights for the promise of attaining fame and fortune as a "true author."

~ ~ ~

It was as if a connection to the "great knower of all" had opened up in his brain. Adam's second book was flowing from him like jazz from Charlie Parker. Each day as he placed his hands on the keyboard, the words, scenarios, plot points, twists, and turns streamed from his fingertips into his word processor. His first book was 285 pages. Now he was well over 400 pages into his second but felt as though he was just halfway through. Imagining the physical weight of his second novel, Adam thought, *I may have more Russian blood in me than previously thought.*

The easy flow of the book served to maintain Adam's positive attitude. The occasional backfires from his publisher—poor cover design, late edits, late galleys—could be dismissed as minor speed bumps on the publishing journey.

Hoping to circumvent some of the delays encountered with his first book, Adam decided to use one of the TPP editors in a private capacity to edit his second novel. It was expensive, and Sarah had begrudgingly transferred the fifteen hundred dollars from their retirement account to the editor. After what seemed like an interminable time, the editor returned a document with more questions than answers.

The editor thought there were really two books in Adam's manuscript and encouraged him to spend his time developing the transition between the two novels. Adam attacked the manuscript with renewed vigor. He was consumed with writing better conclusions for what would be book 1 and book 2 of a series. The summer and fall months slipped away.

The November 1 release date for *Chickens* came and went. All opportunities to produce advance reader copies, conduct pre-release interviews, advertise with influencers—all the tasks that *How to Become a Successful Author* said were necessary before the release of a book—had been bungled by the publisher's inability to produce a physical book by the stated release date.

Adam was becoming obsessive in his feelings about Tontitown Premier Press. His financial relationship with the editor had indeed secured publishing contracts with TPP for his next two books. The wording of the original contract for *Chickens* had locked him into giving TPP the right of first refusal for any books containing any of the characters from the contracted book. Adam was dubious of the publisher at this point. He was seeing complaints from other authors on the publisher's Facebook page and in industry blogs.

"Money talks," Adam reasoned to Sarah at the time. When he asked for a second fifteen hundred dollars to edit the second book in the series, Sarah had reluctantly transferred the money. The deep sigh she exhaled as she made the transfer told Adam her thoughts without saying a word. When the editing of the last book was completed, the editor had gone "right to the top" and secured release dates of January 1 for book 1 and April 1 for book 2.

Not being a young man, Adam knew that his time on earth was limited, as was his ability to continue to form sentences and witty phrases. The timely release of his books was of the highest importance. His dad had died at seventy-eight. While Adam Sr. had led a very unhealthy lifestyle, Adam knew that his dad's ability to articulate had declined rapidly after seventy. Whatever writing career Adam was destined to have was at the mercy of the gods and the TPP scheduling staff. The normal "eighteen months to two years" stated on most publisher's websites was out of the question for him. For some reason, he felt time was of the essence.

~ ~ ~

Nobody Here but Us Chickens was released on November 20, just in time for a limited Christmas season. When Adam opened the box of hardcover copies purchased from the publisher's bookstore at a 45 percent discount, the joy overwhelmed him. Seeing the cover that he helped design, the dedication, and the acknowledgments to all the people who had made the book possible bound together in an actual book of his words was almost more than he could bear. When Sarah read the dedication out loud, "To Sarah, who made all things possible," the tears in her eyes made Adam forget about the ten author's copies that he was supposed to receive for free. He would have been happy to pay retail to see the pride in his wife's eyes.

Adam had made all the preparations for his book's release that were in the contract and on the publisher's web page. He had set up a web page in his own name. A private person, Adam had always pooh-poohed people who had to chronicle every sneeze, every bug bite with strangers on the internet. Against his better instincts, Adam had set up a Facebook page and was sure that he had more "friends" in Africa than Mandela. He scoured the internet for ways to promote his book and found very few free options. Reviews from readers appeared to be the golden fleece for an author. How to obtain those reviews was the question that Adam was once again posing to Sarah over lunch.

"I just don't know how it's possible for a book that's just been released to have a hundred reviews on the day it comes out," Adam said as he reached for the soup ladle. "How'd they get the book? Who coordinated the advance reader copies, or whatever it is, to get this many people to not only read the book but to write a review of it? It just doesn't seem like I'm doing something right, and I've tried to do everything I've been told."

"I'm sure you have, honey," Sarah said, passing the bread. "Maybe these big publishers have paid reviewers, people that just read the publisher's books and write reviews on them."

"I'm not sure that's how it works," Adam replied. "But wouldn't that be a cush job? Just reading books and writing about them? I don't know, I hate to give out books and ask everyone to write a review. Your family has been very good about leaving reviews—thank you—but what do I do next to get more readers? I see some of the TPP authors have done what's called book trailers."

"What's that?" Sarah asked.

"It's like a movie preview except for a book," Adam answered. "It shows action scenes from the book that hopefully make a prospective reader go, 'Oh yeah, I want to read that.'"

"That sounds expensive. How much would something like that cost?"

"Well, they go from a hundred dollars to the thousands of dollars," Adam said. "I could try one of the cheaper versions first and see how it goes, if you think I'm not making too big a deal of it. I do have two more books coming out, and buying books for friends and family is liable to set us back a thousand dollars or so."

Sarah's eyebrow rose an inch on her face, but she controlled her emotions. She bit her lower lip and seemed to choose her words carefully before speaking. "And I guess the new books will need promoting too?"

Adam sheepishly turned away from his wife. "Yeah, I mean, it wouldn't be right, would it, to not give them the same chance that we've given *Chickens*. It might not be as bad as you think because we'll be promoting a series instead of two individual books."

"OK, whatever you think," Sarah said as she got ready to leave for work. "I'm going to go in a little early today. They're offering up to ten hours of overtime a week now at the hospital, so I'll take advantage of it while I can."

Adam crossed the room to his wife and put his arm around her shoulders.

"I couldn't do it without you, you know. You are my everything, and someday soon we'll look back at this and laugh.

It seemed as though *Chickens* had found a place to roost, and it was not at the top of the bestseller list. Equally as important in Adam's mind was the fact that the New Year had not brought the release of his second novel. He had not received the galleys or even a cover. Constant calls and emails to the owner of what Adam knew now was a three-woman operation had driven Adam's blood pressure to stratospheric levels. Excuses were compounded by excuses.

In a fit of desperation, Adam called the editor who had taken three thousand dollars of their hard-earned money and demanded that she deliver on her promise. She was apologetic but offered no hope of being able to move the owner, who was revealed to be a "vindictive person." Adam learned that "once you get on the wrong side of her" you would be bludgeoned by the contract into oblivion. He realized in that moment that his works might never see the light of day.

"I've got some news," he began the conversation at lunch that day. "I talked to Cammy at TPP, and she seemed to think that since nothing has been done on my new books—and she emphasized the word 'nothing'—that I should try to get released from my contract so that I can shop my books somewhere else."

"Do you think that would work?" Sarah asked. "Do you think she'd be willing to give up on you so easily?"

"She might," Adam answered. "*Chickens* isn't making her rich, and she's signed about fifty more authors in the last couple of months, so I'm sure she's got plenty of work to contend with."

"Then what would you do?" Sarah asked, getting up from the table to retrieve napkins. "Would you start sending out submissions and go through all of that anxiety all over again?"

"Maybe. Or maybe I decide to say 'Screw it' to the publishing industry and publish my own stuff," Adam replied. "The one thing that I've learned in the last few months is that except for a very, very select few, authors are in it alone. We're supposed to advertise, set up signings, reviews, and interviews—everything on our own. And for a pittance in royalties, which with TPP aren't even getting paid. If I can get free, I can pursue other publishers while I learn how to self-publish. The rewards are vastly different. Where I'm getting about eighty cents for a hardcover, or supposed to, I'd get $5.85 if I was the publisher. That's a pretty big incentive to self-publish."

"Wow, I didn't know that the difference was that huge," Sarah said. "It sounds like since you're doing all of the work anyway you should get most of the rewards. Has publishing always been like this?"

"I don't think so, and maybe I'm just seeing the worst of what it's become, but I think I need to see if I can get out of my contracts for the new books," Adam said as he took Sarah's plate from the table to the sink. "I need to be in control of my destiny, whatever that is or means."

~ ~ ~

The agreed upon price was a thousand dollars, and two days after the wire transfer was made, Adam received an author's release form from Shani Wilson, the owner of Tontitown Premier Press. Such a simple document, but Adam looked at it as a freed slave may have looked at the Emancipation Proclamation. He was free of the mendacity, parsimony, and arrogance of the publisher that was continuing to sign up new authors as if they were growing on trees.

Adam occasionally reviewed the publisher's Facebook page for news of the organization. He was aghast that they had signed over a hundred new authors since he had originally signed. Each one of these writers had entrusted their dream of being an author to the

Arkansas outfit that so far had paid no royalties to Adam. In posts left by others, Adam could see that the publisher had also abdicated their responsibility to file the proper forms with the government for the authors to complete their taxes. In response to an outpouring of negative posts regarding royalties, tax forms, galleys, release dates, and press packets, the owner decided to air her dirty laundry in public to the millions of potential eyes that could be searching for a publisher. It read:

Hi everyone! I have some important updates, so please read through this post in its entirety before asking me questions.

Contacting me:

My info@tontitownpremier.com email has been reset.

If you or your agent sent a message to me prior to February 2 (even if you sent it to info@), it would be safe to resend that message to me. Anything in the inbox prior to Feb 2 was not retained when the ISP suspended my email acct.

As of this posting, my Gmail has 2,397 emails. I will go through those to find anything from bookstores or others who are not in our group.

"Holy cow!" Adam said out loud. "She's admitting to having 2,400 unanswered emails!"

He continued to read further to find promises of hiring additional staff to process the plethora of new writers that the owner had put under contract. Galleys, cover art, and edits would get done in a more or less first in first out manner, unless someone had an "urgent" need.

The epistle quickly detoured from what the publisher could do for the author to what the authors needed to do for the publisher. "Understanding" was key. The publisher had been sick and had not fully recovered from her illness. "Mean" emails demanding things, even if they were in the contract, sent the publisher back to her bed where she sometimes hid for days under the covers. The publisher was convinced that her weight gain was due to the unnecessary stress of having to deal with people's unrealistic demands. Chronic fatigue, bloat, dizziness, and neuropathy were all conditions that the publisher traced back to the unreasonable demands of the authors.

"Jesus Christ," Adam swore aloud. "She's blaming us for everything except the Kennedy assassination."

Adam continued to scroll down the over 1,200-word diatribe to learn of the death of Shani's dog, her compulsive cleaning disorder, the erratic support she received from family and friends, and how the "paper shortage" and "supply chain issues" were preventing the publisher from getting her job done on those days that she felt well enough to peek her head out from under the covers.

Adam read the post twice to be sure he was not imagining what he was reading. The publisher of hundreds of books by hundreds of authors was admitting publicly her malfeasance. He didn't know whether to laugh or cry. Since the comments were left open, he decided to try his luck by shaming her publicly: *So sorry about your troubles. When will I receive my royalties for last year and a 1099 to file my taxes? Thanks.*

He posted the comment, and over the coming days realized that there were other TPP authors that had been pushed so far that it overcame their fear of retribution. Dozens of replies and new comments peppered the TPP Facebook page. Adam had to admit that some of the comments were very mean-spirited, but he could also feel the authors' pain. To put your heart and soul into a project, spending thousands of dollars that you couldn't afford to promote a work that would only return a pittance on was maddening, literally and figuratively.

One particular author, Leonard Bruce, had an especially snarky wit and posted laugh-out-loud comments on the FB page, blasting TPP for their ineptitude. His book was flying off the shelves, and he was trying to determine which advertising methods were the most productive. *Knowing that the dog died from Sonic's tater tots doesn't help me plot my ad spend*, Leonard commented.

Adam chuckled out loud while he nodded his head in agreement. It was time to formulate a plan to gain some control back from the publisher. Maybe some of the other commenters, these renegade authors, might be able to help.

~ ~ ~

Adam spent the next few days navigating the websites of the two biggest-publisher-printers, the same ones TPP used. He was impressed with how easily one could track the sales of their books. Sales were displayed by day, and it would be very easy to match sales to advertising spent to know the effectiveness of the ads. He also learned that paying royalties was a simple matter of sitting down for a couple of hours and just doing it. The data was all there—there were no mysteries, no secret handshakes, no riddles to solve except one. When will Shani Wilson, owner of Tontitown Premier Press, pay her people?

Advertising had been one of the areas of contention between Adam and Shani. Adam wanted to see the daily sales of his book, something only the publisher could see. Shani did not have the time or the inclination to share daily sales with Adam. He had spent four thousand dollars in an effort to promote *Chickens*. It was four thousand dollars that he had taken as an advance on his life insurance policy. He couldn't bring himself to ask Sarah for any more money for what was now becoming his addiction. It ate at him inside to be hiding this secret, but he rationalized that when he died, who would care about four thousand dollars more or less?

"Mikey Ford called me at work yesterday. He wanted to know how you were doing." Sarah shuffled the casserole from the stove to the table. "I told him fine. He acted like he wanted to talk some more but we had a code blue, and I didn't have time for chitchat. Do you have any idea why he was calling?"

Mikey Ford had been their insurance agent for forty years. Apparently, he felt that the long-term relationship embodied him with special powers to pry into his clients' personal lives.

"Nope. He was just probably trying to sell more insurance. You know how those guys are—Always Be Closing." Adam offered the line from one of their favorite movies as an explanation. He prayed the incident would be passed off and that Sarah wouldn't feel the need to investigate further.

Sarah didn't have the time to investigate further. Since the first of the year, she had been working the night shift, from eleven in the evening to seven in the morning. While the change in schedule afforded the couple breakfast together and an early dinner, it turned the rest of the couple's days upside down. To make matters worse, the schedule was creating a visible decline in Sarah's health. She was tired all the time and had been getting crushing migraines. Adam couldn't understand the hospital's use of their most fragile personnel on the most debilitating schedule, but there it was.

As they flipped the calendar over to March, the couple commented to each other that Sarah was exactly six months from a full retirement with excellent benefits. September 1 would be her last day at the hospital.

Unfortunately, she qualified for the ultimate benefit at two that following morning. While checking a patient's IV, Sarah suddenly dropped to the floor and lay undiscovered for over an hour. A code blue was pointless. She was gone.

Adam was inconsolable. Adam and Sarah were childless and without any close relatives. He was now completely alone. Alone with his thoughts. Thoughts that were getting darker and darker every day.

~ ~ ~

To hide from the grief and the guilt, he kept his mind occupied by completing his series. He managed to self-publish the books with very little trouble. Dozens and dozens of informative videos were available to help a newbie with the process. And dozens and dozens of people on the internet were willing to part with their expert advice for a fee. The fees weren't the issue so much as the fact that Adam associated the expenditures of his writing "hobby" with adding to the stress on Sarah. His mind was constantly filled with the *what ifs*.

What if he had not given in to his lifetime vanity of thinking he could be an author? Would Sarah still be with him? *What if* she hadn't felt the need to work overtime to compensate for Adam's drain on their finances? Would she be upstairs waiting for him to come join her for lunch? The *what ifs* plagued him like the leak under the kitchen sink that he never could quite get around to fixing. The *what ifs* drip, drip, dripped.

Eventually Adam became convinced that it was not his desire to write that was the problem, the cause of Sarah's death. It was the failure of Tontitown Premier Press to make his work successful. In Adam's mind, had *Chickens* been promoted properly, it would have sold enough copies to at least pay for the advertising he had purchased. If promoted properly, maybe it would have been a bestseller and Sarah could have retired early. They could have retired to the beach like Sarah always wanted. If only TPP had done their job.

As Adam looked at TPP's web page and reviewed the authors' comments on their Facebook page, he saw a pattern that to him was unmistakable. TPP was a vanity press. Not one in the traditional manner in which the author pays for the publisher's services up front, but in the manner of a vanity press with no down payment. The publisher would receive remuneration from whatever sales the author was able to create on their own. The fact that TPP was no longer paying royalties bore out his theory. The nonpayment, due to a myriad of excuses that included a dead dog, reinforced the fact to Adam that he, and two hundred other authors, had been scammed. An elaborate scam perpetrated by a single entity. Was Shani Wilson even a person? Had everyone been catfished by an incel living in his parent's basement? Adam meant to find out.

~ ~ ~

The drive to Tontitown, Arkansas, was uneventful. Starting on Sunday afternoon and driving all night had put Adam at his destination at seven the next morning. Adam was surprised that there was no visible motel in Tontitown. The main drag consisted of an unorganized series of businesses without a cohesive theme. This was not Carmel, California. No, Tontitown was miles of farmland with little disparate businesses housed in trailers or strip malls that sprung from the ground like mushrooms as the need for a new service was recognized. Adam determined that the need to house overnight guests had not become an issue. He used his cell phone to book a room in nearby Springdale. "No, he didn't know how long he would be staying.", he told the reservations operator, and he truly didn't know, He was staying until he had satisfaction, whatever that meant.

Driving once around the metal building at the physical address of the publisher, he could see that it was an outer shell that housed a series of storage spaces marked *A* through *K* for identification. Adam parked in the Sonic lot across the street and waited for activity from unit C. He waited all day for anyone to enter or leave the building. His wait for Shani was futile but not altogether without amusement. Adam used the opportunity to sample the Sonic's tater tots that Shani had written so fondly about in her musings.

Fearing a loss of his reservation, Adam drove in the twilight to his motel. The Hampton Inn in Springdale was nicer than most. Adam surmised that the home office of Walmart in nearby

Bentonville created plenty of spillover guests for the motel. He booked the room for a week. While he didn't have an exact plan, he didn't want a snafu with accommodations to affect his mission. After unpacking, he called the front desk.

"May I have a six a.m. wake-up call?"

"Of course," the desk clerk answered. "Would you like repeat calls in case you fall back asleep?"

"No, just the one will do, thank you."

Adam's sleep was fitful, and he answered the wake-up call on the half ring. He couldn't decide whether it was better to grab something from the breakfast buffet or better to give the appearance of having a reason for being in Sonic's parking lot that early in the morning. He opted for Sonic.

After the first day of his stakeout, he thought it prudent to "tip" the day person working behind the counter to ignore his presence. The fact that Adam was homesteading in the fast-food emporium's parking lot was explained by the thinnest of stories: Adam was a "private eye" hoping to get some evidence for a case he was working on. Adam reasoned that eating there at least once a day should have bought him some autonomy, but he wanted to ensure it. The ten-spot and the made-up story seemed to give the counter jockey all the impetus he needed to ignore Adam's presence. The food was at the zenith of "bad for you" fast food, but it would only be for a little while. *It won't be Sonic's food that will prove my undoing*, he thought while crunching on the greasy, empty nothingness of a tater tot.

Friday morning brought rain and a visitor to unit C. Adam was just returning from the bathroom in Sonic when the suspect appeared. The pudgy shape in a floral raincoat fiddled with the keys briefly before unlocking the door. Adam might have missed her if she hadn't had trouble negotiating the door with her fully opened umbrella.

Adam was faced with a Gordian knot of a dilemma he had not yet solved: confront the person he presumed to be Shani on-site or follow her to her home? Settling the question for him before he had time to act, the suspect exited the building and got into what looked like a brand-new Ford Expedition.

Adam followed her at a comfortable distance. The driver turned onto the highway to Springdale and continued on to the far side of town. There she turned onto a dirt road that was framed by an arch declaring "Magnolia Farms and Stables" to the passersby on the highway. Adam drove past the sign for about a mile before turning back. He slowed as he came near the sign and looked as deep into the driveway as he could. One of his dilemmas was solved. The confrontation would have to happen at her "place of business." There was no telling what might be waiting for him at the end of that driveway.

Adam returned to the hotel and began to strategize his next moves. He reserved his room "for at least another week" and literally commandeered the office center for the next three days. Searches for "Magnolia Farms and Stables" brought up a tangled web of court filings. Once a proud breeding farm for thoroughbred racehorses, Magnolia Farms was now a puppy mill. Shani Wilson's name appeared on several LLC applications, from insurance agent to real estate agent to life coach. Strangely, there was no business listing for the publishing firm. No LLC, no corporation, nothing. Adam looked up each of the entities on the internet and was surprised to see all the websites shut down except the publishing house and the puppy mill. He was confused by the opulent appearance of the farm and car and what looked like a lot of failed businesses. Convinced that Shani's trip to Tontitown was a once-a-week trip to pick up mail, Adam mentally prepared himself for her next mail run.

~ ~ ~

Friday morning, shortly after ten, the black Ford Expedition pulled into the parking space in front of unit C. The dumpy figure of a woman stepped down from the SUV and collected her handbag and other belongings before attempting to enter the building. The fumbling of keys and paraphernalia gave Adam the time he needed to cross the alleyway between the office and the Sonic. As Shani pushed open the door, Adam pushed in behind her. Giving Shani a quick shove , he cleared enough space behind him to close the door.

"What—what—Who are you?" the spectacled woman sputtered. "I know you. You're Adam what's-his-face. What do you want? What's the meaning of this? You're not supposed to be here without an appointment. What's the meaning of this?"

Adam hadn't decided beforehand whether to brandish the little .25 caliber automatic or not. Now in the heat of the moment and with the outrage displayed by the owner, he decided to gain the upper hand. Pulling the gun from his pants pocket, he raised it slowly and said, "We're going to talk, and you're going to tell the truth. How truthful you are will determine the outcome for both of us. We're either going to be famous for something besides our love of the printed word, or we'll go on with our miserable lives."

"I don't understand. Why did you come all this way to tell me about whatever dispute you think you have?" Shani put her purse on the desk and began to sit down in the large, overstuffed chair. "Why have you come to my place of business when there's any number of civilized ways to contact me?"

Adam flashed on a myriad of TV plots where the confronted sat down behind a desk that allowed them access to a gun or panic button. As Shani sat, Adam pushed the chair back against a wall that was stacked from floor to ceiling with books. Satisfied he could avoid any books flung at him from that distance, he sat on the edge of the desk and surveyed his surroundings. The cheapest pine paneling covered the walls behind stacks and stacks of books. He tried to calculate how many author proofs were scattered about waiting to be sold at retail or 45 percent off to the author. From the looks of things, business was not brisk.

Adam tried to clear the haunting old woman smell of White Shoulders perfume from his nose before he spoke. "Why have I come in person instead of letting my email join the other two thousand emails praying for a response? Why would I not post on social media my personal thoughts about your business practices and who I think you are as a person? Good question."

The edge of the desk was hitting a nerve in his buttocks, causing his lower half to go numb. Adam looked about the office for another chair, one that could be used to entertain a guest, but there wasn't one. Although it left his feet dangling, he pushed himself fully up onto the desk. The change provided a more comfortable seating arrangement and gave him the advantage of looking down on the person whom he believed to be the bane of his existence.

Shani stared back at Adam with the regal haughtiness of a queen. "And what is the source of your malfunction? You wrote a crappy book about crappy people, and now you're upset because it hasn't taken off like a James Michener novel? Or even better, you're upset because your life story isn't being taught in high schools alongside that of Hemingway and Conrad?"

In that moment, Adam realized the answers to his questions didn't matter. Sarah was gone. Truth would not bring her back. Restitution could not be made. Explaining dreams to a reptile served no purpose. He opened his mouth, but the glare from Shani's eyes left him stumbling to make a sound.

"Errgggghh" was all he managed to articulate before creating a small hole between the eyes of the unrepentant publisher.

Ironically, the crack of the small-caliber weapon cleared Adam's mind. "In for a penny, in for a pound," he said to the lifeless publisher. He pulled the can of lighter fluid from his back pocket, doused the desk, and sprayed the fluid into every drawer. He was hopeful that the desk contained the authors' contracts, past and present. It was his belief that when the company dissolved, all his fellow indentured servants would be freed. That was his hope.

The desk burned with a flesh-melting heat. Adam stayed inside the office as long as he could. Shani never moved. Finally, the acrid smoke drove him into the parking lot.

Deciding to let the fire have its way with Shani's body, Adam sat on the ample bumper of Shani's car and called 911. The police arrived five minutes after the volunteer fire department showed up. Like a scene from *Fahrenheit 451*, glimpses into the office revealed piles of books burning. The irony caused Adam to grin as his head was pushed down into the back of the patrol car.

~ ~ ~

The week of his trial, *Nobody Here but Us Chickens* hit the *New York Times* bestseller list. It climbed to number four before sliding back down into mediocrity. Amazon sales were about 450 books a day, which made it TPP's number one seller. Shani's estate garnered the benefits of all of Shani's twisted dealings without having to suffer her personality.

Adam's lawyer contracted with a ghostwriter to finish Adam's series. It was the lawyer's hope that Adam's lingering notoriety would provide enough sales to pay not only the ghostwriter's fees but the lawyer's as well. If there was anything left over, the lawyer promised to fund Adam's commissary account.

Adam was thankful for his lawyer's efforts. The little Royal typewriter he used every day required ribbons, and the balled-up pages of rejected novel required replenishing with fresh paper from the commissary. He knew he had one more story to tell, and he was determined to tell it. He had nothing but time.

ADDIE

Every January and July, furniture and gift buyers from all over the United States descend on local markets to peruse the new offerings from vendors around the world. While there are markets in New York City, Chicago, San Francisco, and Los Angeles, the vast majority of buyers choose to attend the markets hosted in Atlanta and Dallas.

Certainly, the inclement weather in the north explains some of the migration south for the January market. The July crowds can only be attributed to the focus of the movers and shakers of the respective city governments to be seen as the number one spot for conventions and conferences. Dallas and Atlanta compete head-to-head on a macro level, while individual vendors compete in more nuanced ways.

Free lunch and drinks at any time of the day was how the Newton Laine and Associates showroom in Atlanta hoped to maintain their edge over their competition. The appearance of a packed showroom gave the impression to anyone walking by that this was the showroom with the hot lines, the best deals. In point of fact, a lot of the time, the crowds of buyers in the showroom were waiting for spots at the lunch table.

Newcomers fighting their way into the showroom would at some point learn that many of the people reviewing the displays were queued up for a spot "in the back." Showroom greeters would determine which salesperson covered the buyer's territory and introduce them to the potential clients. It was then up to the salesperson to determine whether to take the buyer's orders before or after extending hospitality. A clever salesperson could manage three or four groups at a time with just one assistant and the circling pattern offered by the lunchroom. It was a system maximized for sales.

The manager of the lunchroom also maximized her space to feed the relentless hordes that descended upon her daily. It was up to the manager to shoehorn buyers from disparate parts of the country into the limited space allotted and ensure that the customers left the hospitality area happy. "Happy" might be defined as four sandwiches and/or four Bloody Marys. It was up to Addie Mae Johnson to determine when each customer had reached their point of satiety.

The gargantuan task was managed by a woman four feet, ten inches tall. She seemed even smaller. As dark as night, the contrast to her skin tone was most pronounced when Addie flashed her pearly white teeth in a smile that went from ear to ear. It was as if her whole face became that smile. No one could have that smile beaming on them and not feel welcome.

Lending a sort of twisted comfort to the Southern customers, Addie wore her hair in a mammy-style bandanna. A caricature artist would have portrayed a small Aunt Jemima on his page. If anyone had ever questioned Addie's mode of dress, it was not known. As the saying goes, "If it ain't broke, don't fix it," and Addie worked garbed as she might have a century before.

In spite of being chastened to not accept tips, Addie regularly took the folded bills and slipped them into the pocket of her apron. The owner, Newton Laine, was willing to overlook a few rules to maintain harmony in the back room.

Addie received cursory help from any of the other showroom employees. To the contrary, each salesperson's insistence that their customer be seated next led to inevitable conflicts. The most heated conflicts were resolved by Addie striding directly to the owner and declaring that she was "out of here, never comin' back" if he didn't fix x, y, or z. Addie always won; x, y, or z was immediately fixed to her satisfaction.

One such altercation occurred when the newest member of the sales team asked for his tuna fish sandwich to be on toasted wheat. "A slice of tomato would be nice, too." Addie responded by placing her apron on its hook, gathering her purse, and marching straight to the owner. Newton dropped what he was doing to search for the defendant. He found the new salesperson working with clients. With Addie overseeing, the owner dressed down the young man for his lack of consideration to the "fabulous job" being performed by Addie.

Particularly stung by what he considered to be a loss of status in his confrontation with Addie, the neophyte salesman sought validation from the senior member of the group. The elder listened to the new guy vent and patiently waited for him to finish. At the end of the diatribe the elder salesperson peered over his bifocals in sage-like fashion and replied, "The one thing I learned in the Army was you don't ever mess with the cook. Think about it."

The young man did think about it and vowed to never cross swords with Addie again. In fact, he made sure that any time he was around the bar, making drinks for his customers, he asked Addie if he could fix anything for her. She had always declined, until the next to the last day of the July market. It was late in the afternoon, and Addie asked the young salesman to fix her a glass of ice water.

Eager to please, the new guy filled the paper cup and took it back to the cubby that had been purposed as a kitchen.

"Here's your ice water," he declared proudly.

"Put it on the shelf there. I'll get it in a minute," answered Addie.

Walking back into the lunchroom, he was shocked to hear the choking sounds coming from the cubby. He returned to the kitchen area to see Addie sputtering, her dark black cheeks turning red from the effort.

"What is that?" she sputtered.

"Water, I got you water. You said to fix you a glass of ice water," the salesman replied in a panic.

"Whatcha want, Addie, a glass of ice water?" another sales rep asked.

"That's right, baby. Get Addie a glass of ice water, a big one," Addie said as she continued to stir a bowl of tuna fish salad for the next day's sandwiches. The bowl, filled with tuna fish, boiled eggs, and mayonnaise, must have weighed fifteen pounds. Addie had it secured to her body with one arm while she vigorously stirred with the other.

Rich, the sales rep from Florida, walked over to the bar and put one cube of ice in a paper cup and then filled it nearly to the brim with gin. As he turned back to the kitchen area, he tilted his head back and raised his eyebrows signaling to the new guy that this was what a "cup of ice water" meant to Addie. The new guy nodded his head to acknowledge the new entry to his lexicon. He had often wondered how the little Black woman could maintain her servile attitude dealing with the constant crush of customers and their boorish behavior. Now he had a clue.

The next day was the day of goodbyes and good lucks as the sales team departed for their respective territories. The showroom would still maintain a brisk business through the day, but it was predominately customers within an easy drive. The new salesman would be there until the bitter end. Atlanta was his territory.

As he turned the corner to the bar area, he was confronted by the most strikingly beautiful Black woman he had ever seen. There was no doubt that she was Addie's child, from the darkness of skin tone to the high cheekbones, this apple had not fallen too far from the tree.

She was about five feet, four inches tall, wearing the high heels she was required to wear. Her face was enhanced by the reddest of lipsticks, with rouge accentuating her high cheekbones. She was dressed in a Delta flight-attendant uniform and looked as if she was ready to deliver preflight instructions.

Instead, she was receiving some version of the riot act from her mom. The salesman appeared busy fixing drinks, while trying to gather what insight he could into their personal conversation. He learned that Addie was not pleased with how her daughter had abandoned her child on a regular basis to go "catting around." The daughter tried to explain that she needed to have a social life, which couldn't be just work and come home. They both gave just as good as they took.

As the salesman turned from the bar with his drink order balanced on his clipboard, Addie stepped out of the kitchen area to stand closer to her daughter. She was still holding the gigantic spoon she used to stir the tuna fish and pointed it directly at her daughter's face. Oblivious to the lunchroom filled with customers, Addie stood as close to eye to eye with her daughter as their height differential would allow.

"I brought you into this life and I can take you out, don't you never forget it!" she said with a flourish of the spoon.

Wings could not have carried the young man faster from the area than his feet did at that moment. Returning to his customers, he kept one eye on the customer's order and the other peeled for mayhem. After a bit, he saw the daughter leave the showroom, her dark blue uniform mixing in with the last of the lookie-loos in the hall. If she ever returned to the showroom, he was unaware.

As luck would have it, he spent the next two hours with the same group. While waiting for the orders to be totaled, the owner ushered the group to the hospitality room where they found a very inebriated Addie. Still on the clock, Addie tried to serve the group, but it was a task too great for her condition. She was encouraged to sit in the kitchen area and wait for her husband to pick her up.

Her husband arrived an hour or so later. A thin man, about five feet, eight inches, he seemed to suffer from a severe pigmentation problem. With the help of the owner's wife, Marsha, the husband was able to get Addie down the elevator and to the waiting car in the underground parking.

The young man was sitting in the back with the Florida rep when the owner's wife returned.

"I want to know if either of you are responsible for this," Marsha questioned the pair.

"Responsible, how?" countered Rich.

"Feeding her drinks all day," Marsha answered, eyeing the sales rep curiously. "You know how you like to stir things up."

The new guy decided to skate out onto thin ice. "She was fighting with her daughter earlier. Maybe that's what upset her."

Marsha spun to the young salesman. "And how do you know this?"

"Because I came back to fix drinks, and she was fighting with this young woman in a Delta uniform that was clearly her daughter," he explained. "Addie didn't introduce us, but she was clearly Addie's daughter."

"Hmm," Marsha responded and walked away.

"Her daughter's a looker, ain't she," Rich opined.

"Well, she clearly didn't inherit her dad's skin, if that was her dad picking up Addie," the new guy replied.

"That's her dad, but that ain't a skin condition," Rich offered. "Didn't you hear?"

"Hear what? I feel like somebody should print up a program to let new people know who all of the players are."

"Wouldn't work. The program would be out of date from market to market." Rich leaned in closer. "Addie set fire to him."

The new guy had no verbal response, but his eyes were wide open.

"Yep, he came home drunk one time too many, and Addie thought he'd been playing around. So, she waited until he passed out and soaked him in lighter fluid. Lit the match and—poof!—Addie was a flambé chef."

The new salesman still had no response.

Rich continued. "Addie says he screamed so pitiful that she put it out right away, but the damage was done."

"Didn't he press charges?" the young man asked. "I'd have her locked up for attempted murder and whatever else I could think of."

"Nope," Rich answered. "I guess he figured he had it coming, or . . . he was scared of what she'd do to him when she got out." Rich got up to pour himself a drink. "Addie Mae 'Boom Boom' Johnson. She is a straight razor-totin' woman. Keep that in mind the next time you think about asking her for something that's not on the menu."

His smile was not reassuring.

THE EQUALIZER

The view from his office always took his breath. Looking out over the San Francisco Bay, Luciano Vega could see ships from all over the world bringing goods to the United States in return for the world's standard currency, the US dollar. The view from the forty-eighth floor of the Transamerica Pyramid was outstanding; Luciano's corner office looked out on the bay in one direction and downtown San Francisco in the other.

The intercom interrupted his reverie, and he pushed the button connecting him to the rest of the world.

"Mr. Gettiz is on line one," stated the operator. "Shall I put him through?"

"Of course," Luciano responded. *When does one not take the call of one of the richest people in the world?* he thought. "Mr. Gettiz, how are you?"

"Very well, thank you, and about to get better if this proposal of yours pans out," the voice on the other side of the world answered. "I just have a couple of questions. Do you have your prospectus in front of you?"

"Yes, of course, never leave home without it," Luciano said as he reached for the inch-thick document that had consumed the last three years of his life. What had started as a graduate school project had become his entry into the lucrative oil business. His calculations and prognostications had been spot on. His reward for his predictions was being now ensconced in a luxury high-rise office, counseling a scion of the business world. "What page?"

"Let's start with page eighty-six," the billionaire responded. "If I'm reading this right, you're saying that the recoverable oil lying under the tundra in Siberia is two to three times greater than the Saudi Arabian oil fields?"

"Yes, sir, and that's a conservative estimate," Luciano said. "My friend has been poking holes in a circle around the area that I specified for the last year, and there doesn't seem to be any drop-off in production value as far as he has tested."

"And you think we can do a better job than the Russians getting it out of the ground?"

"Without question. I could pick up two kids on the beach with pails and shovels and do a better job digging for oil than the Russians." Luciano waited for the hearty laugh to subside before continuing. "The real point is not that our recovery methods are so much better than the Russians', it's that I don't think the Russians know that it's there. I mean, I know that they know it's there. I just think that they still think the tundra is still frozen rock hard and that, as sloppy as their operations are, they'd have an easier time of it somewhere else. Remember, this is basically their economy, and they don't want to tie up millions in a long-term project. They want quick cash."

The billionaire interrupted. "Well, son, we all want quick cash. Can't blame the Russkies for that. How are we going to sneak in and steal the fat pig without farmer Ivan pulling out his shotgun?"

"Well, sir, as the first eighty or so pages of my report point out, the world is going through a climate crisis that is unprecedented in man's history. Each succeeding year for the past five years has been hotter than the last. Climatologists don't expect it to improve, possibly not ever. The tundra is thawing at an exponential rate. Methane gas alone will pay back your investment tenfold. If we can polka dot the areas I've outlined with rigs, we'll put ourselves in line to be the company chosen to put in the pipeline for the area. Then we'll make money off of every rig that uses our pipeline to get their gas and oil to market."

"So, Luke"—the capitalist used Luciano's Americanized first name—"all I have to do to put this wildly imaginative idea of yours in place is to give you control of our stock until the London markets open, is that right?"

"Yes, sir, we'll begin shorting our stock on the Nikkei in Tokyo on the morning of D-Day. Our analysts have predicted that by the time Wall Street opens we'll see at least a twenty percent reduction price in cost per share. A few well-placed rumors will drive the price even lower. By the time we make our announcement here in San Francisco of our agreement with the Russians to open up the tundra fields, we should be down twenty-five to thirty percent in market value. We'll swoop in right before the announcement is made and buy everything we can. Once we make our announcement, we should see our stock rise a minimum of ten percent by the opening of the Tokyo markets."

"This sounds so risky," the billionaire said. "If this is so easy, why haven't other companies done it?"

"They do it all of the time," Luciano countered. "You just don't hear about it. Most of the time it's to raise quick capital, sort of like we're doing. Where we're differing is that we know we're about to make an announcement that's going to drive our stock way up. We're taking advantage of this knowledge to gain a larger ownership of a company that is about to skyrocket in value."

"I hear the excitement in your voice, Luke. I'm convinced you're convinced." The billionaire sighed into the phone. "Do you have the agreement with the Russians signed yet?"

"I'll have it by close of business tomorrow," Luciano answered, his eyes glancing over the contract on the top of his desk. "That will put us in place to begin our market manipulation Monday morning. Actually, there will be some drift in the market over the weekend, so we'll hope to affect that before the Nikkei opens."

"Strange world, isn't it, where you're allowed to put bets on a company failing, rather than just betting on its success?" the billionaire asked. "But if we profit like your prospectus predicts, we'd be fools not to use every tool in our toolbox to make our shareholders happy. You have a very successful track record with us, Luke, and I'm betting that you've already made plans for how you're going to spend the big bonus coming through when this pays off. I'll tell our friends and portfolio managers that have less than five percent of our stock to start selling our stock. If asked, the reason will be that we plan on buying back the stock to 'shore up the retirement fund.'"

"Excellent idea, sir," Luciano replied, nervously clicking his ballpoint pen. "Then we'll just let the rumor mill drive down the price until we're ready to announce our Russian venture."

"Very good," Gettiz summed up. "You've been a true diamond in the rough for us, Luke. You continue to prove the genius of my Gettiz International Scholarship Fund. Talk to you soon."

And with that the phone returned to dial tone.

Luciano immediately added a picture of the Andean condor, the national bird of Ecuador, to his Pinterest page, signaling to his compatriot in Russia that the plan was a go. As he gazed on the majesty of the bird, he reflected on the path that had led from the oil fields in Ecuador to the office in San Francisco. He walked to the window and looked down at the street below. The people were scurrying like ants to and fro, completely involved in their daily tasks. Those ants that called Gettiz Oil home were about to have their lives upended if the plan worked, Luciano would be a major contributor to the change.

~ ~ ~

Born in San Carlos, Ecuador, you might say that oil was in Luciano's blood. Sadly, that fact could be said about every resident of San Carlos and the surrounding area. They literally had hydrocarbons in their blood from decades of ground-water contamination. The contamination came from the oil fields sprinkled about the area and their settling ponds that were not handled properly. The incidence of cancer in the area was four times the norm.

Luciano's parents were educated people, his father an oil field engineer and his mother a schoolteacher. His parents were well aware of the hazards and took great pains to have Luciano and his sister, Theresa, avoid the hazards. The family not only drank bottled water but also bathed in it. When other children went tubing in the Mindo River, Luciano and his sister stayed behind. Luciano didn't learn to swim until he went away to boarding school in Quito.

Theresa never got the chance to learn to swim or get a higher education. On her twelfth birthday, Theresa's mom found a disturbing knot on Theresa's head as she was putting the "queen for a day" crown on her daughter. Tests proved the family's worst fears. Theresa was riddled with tumors. Luciano was encouraged to stay in school, to continue his education rather than come home and watch his sister waste away. Theresa was gone before ever becoming a teenager. Distraught, the Vegas joined in the fight against the oil company that they blamed for the death of their daughter, Gettiz Oil.

The suit carried on for years while the oil company bought politician after succeeding politician to delay or dismiss the suit. Finally, a reformer came into power who couldn't be bought. Hundreds of families had joined the suit, and while not every victim died, they all suffered a severe loss of quality of life. The land was no longer arable, the water was unfit to drink, and the stench from the oil fields was overpowering. Those who could move from the area did, but they knew that they carried a ticking time bomb within them. No matter where they relocated, the cancer bomb would eventually explode.

The litigation went forward in spite of the fact that it was moved to an international court in New York City. While the jury was deciding the fate of the litigants, Gettiz sold their Ecuadorian holdings to Texas Oil. Gettiz's subsequent arguments for not paying the judgment meted out by the international court was that they had sold all assets and liabilities to Texas Oil. Texas Oil countered with the argument that, at the time of purchase, the liabilities did not exist and were therefore not part of the deal. Lawyers for both sides kept the suits going for years while the litigants continued to die without relief.

Luciano's parents moved to Quito to be near their surviving child while they awaited relief from the court system. Luciano graduated at the top of his class and was astounded when he received his acceptance package from Harvard University. He suspected that his strong essay about his sister's illness and the plight of his hometown had helped gain his entry into one of the foremost business schools in the world. A 4.0 average put him in line to be considered for the prestigious Gettiz International Scholarship at the Sorbonne in Paris.

He was in Paris working on his doctorate in finance when the news came that his father's health was declining. He made it to the hospital in time to catch his father's last conscious moments. "Corrige una injusticia," the elder whispered into his son's ear before falling into the sleep that takes us all. "Right this wrong."

The news of his mother's passing reached him on the day that his dissertation, "Oil Exploration, Corporate Liquidity, and Asset Prices," was delivered. His anxiety about the acceptance of his doctorate gave way to the crushing grief of the loss of his mother. On the plane ride home, he reflected on the stoicism of the mother that would not let her health get in the way of her son's achievements. *Corrige una injusticia*, he thought.

The call from the Gettiz Oil Company offering him a job came as a bit of a surprise. The meeting with the old man in Rome was disarming. Luciano had expected a hydra rather than a kindly, balding old man bedecked in cargo shorts and huaraches. For some reason there was an instant connection, and when the old man promised, "I've got my eye on you," Luciano knew that he meant it.

Despite living in Italy and speaking fluent Italian, the old man chose to speak in English and to call Luciano "Luke." Luciano didn't let the attempt at kinship fluster or flatter him. In fact, he hoped to use the friendship to his advantage in every way he could. He was in a very competitive business with the brightest of minds vying for the top positions. Luciano hoped to beat them all there.

He began his career in London, overseeing Gettiz's North Sea holdings. Being a small stakeholder in the vast area of the North Sea gave Luciano the opportunity to learn on the job and to learn firsthand how the fluctuation in oil production affected the world's markets. Though Gettiz operated just two offshore rigs, Luciano learned quickly how production could be throttled or opened up based off of price. More importantly, he learned how the financial reports could be manipulated to present the company's assets in the most favorable light. Since the debacle in Ecuador and the sale to Texas Oil, Gettiz had become a bit of a market pariah, as though there was a line that even big oil wouldn't cross. The line was saddling another "oil brother" with your cleanup. Luciano knew from experience that there wasn't always honor among thieves.

It was in London that Luciano met Mary. Mary was a botanist and truly the most beautiful, intelligent woman Luciano had ever encountered. When he told her that he was from San Carlos, Mary delivered an hour-long speech about the destruction of the flora and fauna in the Amazon basin. As a result of the speech, Luciano was less than forthcoming about his career. For the longest time he told Mary that he worked in "finance," without mentioning the firm. Eventually the truth had to come out; his feelings for the bright-eyed savior of the planet could not be denied. Confident that he had met his life partner, Mary was the first person Luciano confided in about his plan to "corrige una injusticia."

"I don't know how yet," he told her. "I just know that it has to be done. Someone must put an end to this evil."

On their second anniversary, Mary brought home the news that she was pregnant. She lovingly referred to the embryo as a "pea pod" during their first sonogram. Thereafter, Luciano took delight in asking his wife on a daily basis, "Mary, Mary, how does your garden grow?" It seemed to grow quite well until the six-month checkup. The doctor became visibly alarmed at the display on the sonogram. The "pea pod" had developed additional appendages and a severe splitting of the cranium. Fearing the worst of outcomes for the mother and the child, the doctor recommended that the pregnancy be terminated.

A ceremonial burial for Luciano's son was held in a little town outside of London. The drive to the little town for his weekly visits helped temper Luciano's anger at his loss. His family had now lost their bloodline; there would be no more Vegas from his ancestors. The oil in his blood had bubbled to the surface in the worst possible way. Professional counseling brought Luciano and Mary to the point where they agreed that they might adopt someday. "But first," Luciano told Mary, "I want to throw every fiber of my being into this mission." Mary agreed, and Luciano was unstoppable in his quest to attain a position where he could "corrige una injusticia."

His rise to the top of Gettiz was phenomenal. Many detractors floated rumors about Luciano's "special relationship" with the old man, but the proof of his skill was in the quarterly reports. No one could deny the numbers. Gettiz Oil was more financially stable than it had ever been. The shareholders were as happy as swine at the trough. At the annual meetings Luciano continued to show the same humility with the congregation of millionaires as he had with his classmates at Harvard and the Sorbonne. No one suspected the sheep in wolf's clothing that circulated among them. In fact, many of the scions of business who attended the annual meeting had corporations that needed a financial wizard of their own. More than one had approached Luciano to make a change. Luciano always replied, "No, I am happy where I am doing what I am supposed to be doing."

The friends he had made at the prestigious universities came from different levels of economic backgrounds. There were those lucky enough to have the intelligence and work ethic to rise above their roots, like Luciano. Conversely, there were those born with a silver spoon in their mouth but aware that wealth disparity was not healthy for a democracy or the planet. These friends would be the ones that Luciano counted on the most when the time was right. These well-heeled friends regularly moved vast sums of money without blinking an eye. Their connections would keep them from scrutiny should any component of Luciano's plan fall into legal difficulties. The hour was growing closer.

~ ~ ~

The contract from Gazprom, the Russian state-owned oil company, arrived on Thursday morning. Using an in-house Russian-speaking attorney, Luciano listened carefully to paragraph 24, subcategory A. This was the specific piece of legalese that spelled out the benchmarks for breaking ground and the penalties to be incurred if the benchmarks weren't met. The English-translated version presented to Mr. Gettiz for approval gave the company a much more relaxed timeline. Luciano was relieved when the old man didn't ask for the Russian version of the contract. The inability to meet the contract's demands was a major component of Luciano's plan. The signed version was faxed back to Gazprom, and the first element of the plan was in place.

Posting an American eagle nesting high up a tree on his Pinterest page, Luciano signaled his coconspirators around the world that the first part of the plan was active. Individuals and portfolio managers sympathetic to Luciano's cause started selling off Gettiz stock. By Friday at noon the sell-off was noticeable enough to bring comment on the CNBC noon report. Luciano's former classmate furrowed his brow deeply as he looked into the camera and delivered the news that the sell-off was worldwide. The market guru came back to the Gettiz story at the end of his show to dramatically slam his hand down on the vastly oversized Sell button on his desk. Half a million viewers of the show got the message as "SELL!" was flashed across the screen. The stock had dropped 25 percent by the close of business.

Luciano put Mary on the flight to Quito that evening. For months they had been preparing for this day. Their money was safely hidden by friends in the banking industry. The couple planned to spend their riches and the rest of their days correcting the excesses of capitalism.

"Te amo," Luciano told Mary as they said their goodbyes at the security checkpoint.

"Te amo tambien," Mary responded. "Y corrige una injusticia."

Luciano smiled at his wife and hugged her tightly. "Muy bien, vaya con Dios."

He was still awake when he received Mary's message that she had safely arrived in Quito. Luciano slept that night in the deep sleep of a steel worker after a sixteen-hour shift. Sleep would be precious in the days to come.

~ ~ ~

The Nikkei slippage was better, or worse depending on your point of view, than expected. Gettiz was down by 30 percent at the opening of the Tokyo market. By the time London opened, the stock was down another 10 percent. Wall Street opened with Gettiz Oil at

50 percent of its former value. Luciano wondered if the opening bell, rung by yet another tech start-up, would prove to be the death knell for Gettiz Oil.

Luciano arrived at work promptly at 6 a.m. on D-Day. His array of monitors was tuned to the market in Tokyo, London, and New York. At 6:20 a.m., 3:20 p.m. Rome time, his cell phone rang. It was the old man.

"Luke, I'm scared your plan is working too well," the billionaire stated with a notable sound of concern in his voice. "If this continues, I'm worried about our ability to buy back all of our stock."

"Please don't alarm yourself needlessly," Luciano replied. "When we make our announcement about the deal with the Russians, the stock will rebound rapidly. The company will gain back its value in a couple of days, and then you will have almost complete control of the company and its profits."

"I know that is the plan, but I still worry," the old man said. "I know you know what you are doing, but I still worry."

"Don't worry," Luciano replied as the opening bell was rung on Wall Street. "My plan is working perfectly."

And it was. As the day wore on, the stock dropped to one-third of its original value. By 2 p.m. EST, the old man had used all of Gettiz's cash reserves to buy back his outstanding stock. The buyback should have set off interest from other speculators in purchasing an undervalued stock, but the talking head at CNBC had taken a particular interest in Gettiz Oil. At the end of his noon commentary, he hit the Sell button with such ferocity that he knocked it from its mooring. Not wanting to be caught foolish, all the savvy investors unloaded Gettiz Oil from their portfolios. The announcement of the Russian deal was made from the San Francisco headquarters at noon PST before the markets closed in New York.

With the announcement of the Russian deal made, Gettiz went all out. He used every asset he could leverage to purchase all his outstanding stock. Gettiz refinery, Gettiz rigs, Gettiz tankers—all were used as security. The billionaire even pledged his personal property including his pied-à-terre in New York City. He was all in. He borrowed every nickel he could from every lender willing to listen about the untold riches of the Russian tundra. The old man was primed for a tidal wave of investment from speculators when the deal was delivered on air. The reaction was more like a slow mountain stream. The stock had risen just 5 percent from its lowest point by the close of day.

Luciano listened intently to the voice half a world away.

"Luke, are you sure this going to work? I've bet everything on this, even my house and my Fifth Avenue apartment. When will we see investors come back into the market?" the old man said in a voice tinged with fear.

"Don't worry, sir. When the analysts have time to evaluate the deal we've made with the Russians, they'll come flocking back to us like bees to honey," Luciano said as he watched the first protesters hit the streets on RT, Russia's CNN. Carrying signs in English and Russian, the protesters were letting the Kremlin know that they weren't happy with the exploitation of their wilderness, certainly not by Western concerns.

"We'll be fine," Luciano assured the billionaire. "I'm going to stay right here until the Nikkei opens. We should start seeing the first signs of the pendulum swinging back our way then."

"Fine, fine. Call me no matter what the hour if things aren't going as you planned," Mr. Gettiz implored. "I doubt that I will be sleeping, but if so, have them wake me."

The line went dead without so much as a ciao or goodbye.

Gettiz stock had dropped from $109 a share to just under $36 a share in a day. The old man had hocked everything he owned to purchase back most of his company's outstanding stock at a fantastically low price. According to Luciano's prospectus, all they had to do was to wait for the stock to rise again. The announcement of the deal with the Russians should push their stock price past its previous high and provide all the liquidity needed to explore the tundra. Borrowing money would be easy if the stock returned to just half of its former value and the banks were given an interest in the Russian fields. Risky business, but that was the oil business.

Like the previous day, Gettiz Oil opened lower on the Tokyo market. The slide continued into London. When the bell rang in New York City, the stock was under $35 a share. At 9 a.m. EST the call from Rome came through to Luciano.

"What have you done?" the old man screamed into the phone.

"Sir, please, don't worry. Everything will be OK. The market had a bad day. Everyone took a hit from the Feds raising interest rates. We've just got to be patient and stick to our guns," Luciano said in his most consoling voice. "We've got to stay the course."

"Harrumph" was the response followed by a dead line.

At 2 p.m. San Francisco time, a fax arrived at the Gettiz Oil home office. The fax stated that the Russian partners wanted to exercise their option in paragraph 24 of the contract to accelerate the timeline. The reason given was the widespread opposition of the Russian people to the deal. The Russian partners felt that breaking ground immediately would render the protests moot. The Russian's fax and subsequent phone conversation demanded that Gettiz Oil break ground in thirty days or be prepared to pay the $150,000 a day fine for nonperformance. Luciano waited until the close of Wall Street to phone his boss with the news.

"How will we be able to comply with their demands in such a short time?" Mr. Gettiz queried. "Is your team anywhere near ready to drill?"

"They're physically ready," Luciano responded. "We have the men we need, but there's no modern equipment in the area, just the junk the Russians use."

"Break ground with the Russian equipment while I move heaven and earth to get modern equipment to the area," the billionaire said. "I may have to pledge all of my stock as security for the equipment and logistics, but that's where we are. In for a penny, in for a pound."

In another circumstance Luciano might have admired the old man's bravado in risking it all, gambling everything on a deal, but not this man. Luciano knew the old man would stand on the mast of the sinking ship until his head finally went under water. Sticking to his guns was the old man's forte, even if the guns were aimed at innocents.

"Will do, sir. I'll call my man and have him start on the least productive site first since we'll want to save the better sites for the better equipment."

"Good. You do that while I try to sell what's left of my soul to the bankers."

Gettiz hung up. Luciano looked at the dead phone for a minute before calling his friend in Moscow to start moving whatever equipment he could scrape together to the furthermost claim.

In the best of times, it would take a month to get on site and set up. This was the middle of a particularly vicious Siberian winter. The trucks were halfway to the site when the $150,000 a day nonperformance fee kicked in. After sixty days, Gettiz Oil owed the Russians $9 million in penalties. Adding insult to injury, large interest payments were due to the banks for facilitating the old man's stock buyback. Curiously, the banks had not been interested in financing the oil company's speculative fields in a country that was going through significant political turmoil.

In the end, Gettiz Oil had to sell their rights to the claims in the tundra to one of their competitors. "One of the seven sisters was able to help a brother out," was how the CNBC financial expert succinctly synopsized the event. The company's mismanagement had continued to drive the Gettiz stock down, and the once proud billionaire owed far more than he was worth. Assorted bankruptcy courts around the world would be busy for years sorting it all out.

Luciano had of course been fired, but not before seeing his plan come to fruition. Gettiz Oil was done.

Does it matter if the final blow comes on a Tuesday or Wednesday? It does not, Luciano thought as he gazed out of his office window in Quito. The sign on the door said "Corrige una injusticia."

WRITER'S BLOCK

The author known to millions as Hillary Bruchette Adams sat down at his computer and stared at the twenty-one-inch monitor. The solitary eye of the monitor stared back at him maliciously. *The quick brown fox jumped over the lazy dog* filled the screen as the bestselling author tried to jog his brain into creativity. Try as he might, the fingers that had pounded out six bestsellers in the Fiona Byrne series would not respond. The quick brown fox continued to jump over the lazy dog until the screen ran out of display. Disgusted with himself, the author turned off his monitor and leaned back in his chair.

The chair, a Recaro Titan, was a gift from his publisher after his first book sold a million copies. The author had blamed his lack of progress with his second novel on back pain.

"I can't just sit for twelve hours a day every day in the same position and type," he had complained to his publisher.

His publisher had responded with the chair, and a crew that adjusted the height and pitch of the seat to the optimum levels for comfort. There could be no physical excuses offered or allowed to alter the anticipated spring release date of the second in the Fiona Byrne series, *My Surrender*.

His genre was loosely described as romance. The "bodice busters," as they were known, targeted a segment of the population that was given to fantasy romance. In the author's opinion, the readers were a group of people who found soft cozy-mystery, summer-beach reads too challenging. His first book, *My Challenge*, had been written as a personal objective, a bucket-list item. Writing was something he had wanted to do all his life. His plan was to write a somewhat historical novel about his grandmother's journey to America. He thought that the story of a pretty red-haired, brown-eyed girl from Ireland arriving unaccompanied to Ellis Island was an important one. Being marginalized by everyone because she was a woman was his grandmother's challenge. It was a story that he hoped would be read by his daughter and granddaughters with pride. He was delighted when a publisher agreed with him. The joy of his partial-acceptance letter was meted by the changes the editor was asking for. What had started as a tale of courage told with pride by a grandson was turned into a tale of a girl using her physical attributes, and a quick mind, to manipulate men to her bidding.

He reminded himself that it was an opportunity to do better things in the future and threw himself into the edits. With the final manuscript submitted, he awaited the galleys. When he saw the cover design, he was crushed. *Lurid* was the word that kept blinking like a broken neon sign in his mind. He didn't answer his publisher's emails for three days. The FedEx package arrived from the publisher announcing a possible suit for breach of contract. The author responded by calling the publisher. After a heated back and forth, he decided to go ahead with the publication but only under the provision that the publisher use a pen name. Hillary Bruchette Adams was born that day. There is an irony in the circumstance of embarrassing births, but the author tried not to dwell on it too much.

The first book broke all records for his genre. The publisher wanted to keep the ball rolling and started scheduling what seemed like every aspect of the author's life. The author soon discovered that book tours, interviews, and all of the hoopla involved in promoting a book left him little energy to write. Worn out at the end of the day in motels scattered across the country, he found that there just wasn't the time necessary to concentrate. But in spite of the whirlwind flying about him, he continued to write. He explained to his family that he was "under contract," that he "had to deliver." And he did.

His second book, *My Surrender*, sold out its first edition almost immediately. He had hoped the success of his first book would allow him to turn away from the salacious nature of the genre and to write something more meaningful. In little bits and pieces, he attempted to make his character less floozy, more urbane. His edits would come back from the publisher with large chunks of substitutions. The author had designed his plots to have his character use her mind to navigate the world. The editor would red-line large sections of the manuscript and offer suggestions that would invariably steer Fiona to a swarthy male of questionable repute. The fight was exhausting. The constant promotion was exhausting. Finally, the author quit fighting for his character. Like the title of the book, the author would refer to the time as "My Surrender."

After the success of his second book, the author could have rested on his laurels and piles of cash. He chose instead to see how far he and his public would go to follow Fiona. Each day as he sat down to write he would perform a ritual. He would place his hands on each side of his jaw and make a motion as if he were lifting his head from his neck. He would then place the imaginary head on his desk, saying, "I won't be needing this." And that was how he approached his writing. His contempt for his situation was primarily for his publisher and her harpy editors, but there was self-loathing mixed in as well. He shamelessly watched Univision TV and stole plot lines directly from the telenovelas. No one seemed to notice, much less care. The subsequent four novels were all bestsellers. It worked until it didn't.

His version of writer's block came when he realized he had used all the plots from Spanish TV. He switched to American soap operas only to find out they were all the same plots. He vaguely remembered that Kurt Vonnegut had been pilloried when he had said that there were only three, or maybe it was eight, story "shapes." Either way, according to one of the literary masters, there was not a lot of "new" going on in literature. Based off the quick brown fox's progress in jumping over the lazy dog on his monitor, there would be nothing new going on with Fiona that day. Hillary Bruchette Adams decided to pack it in for the day. Rory O'Connor rose from his chair.

Rory climbed the stairs to the first level. As he climbed, he surveyed the San Fernando Valley through the house's glass-encased southern exposure. When the family moved from Boston to be nearer to "the industry" he had described the house as "ten thousand square feet without a soul." Finding no one in sight in the open floor–plan house, he walked out into the garage. The Mercedes Maybach was missing, which meant that his wife, Trudy, had already embarked on her daily mission of emptying the shops on Rodeo Drive of their wares.

Rory climbed into his 1968 Mustang replica of Steve McQueen's *Bullitt* car and drove slowly down the mountainside. He stayed well within the speed limit. He knew what the car was capable of, but he was also aware of his capabilities. "As a race car driver, I'm a great writer," he would tell those who questioned his lack of interest in seeing what the car "could really do."

He exited the 101 onto Fountain Avenue and drove east toward the Children's Hospital. Two blocks from the hospital he pulled into the parking lot of the penultimate manifestation of a dive bar. The building seemed to be held together by rusty nails, duct tape, and the legend that Charles Bukowski used to start his mornings there.

The narrative was that Bukowski would still be there at closing time most days. As Rory's eyes attempted to adjust to the light, his nose processed the smells of hundreds of bodies exhaling their bodily wastes. These smells had accumulated and clung to all the surfaces of the bar. It was as if a millennium of human decay was trapped inside the walls of the hole-in-the-wall bar.

Rory took a seat at the bar, near the end. To his utter amazement there was a large brass spittoon on the floor beneath the bar rail. His mind raced as he imagined who might have performed what bodily function into the spittoon. He opened a tab with his credit card and ordered a beer. The sight of a credit card seemed to draw interest from a couple of characters in the corner. One of them rose to sit on the stool next to Rory. It was then that Rory realized that his assessment of the smells of the bar might have been wrong. The character next to him seemed to possess all the accumulated smells of humanity that Rory had attributed to a millennium of the promotion of alcoholic spirits.

"Buy a vet a beer?" the disheveled character asked.

"Sure," Rory responded.

"How about my buddy? He served too."

"Why not," Rory answered as he motioned to the bartender. "Where'd you boys serve?"

"Me, I was in Nam. Willy, hell, I don't know, one of the 'Stans. Pakistan, Afghanistan, some other 'Stan. They're all the same," the veteran offered as he tipped his glass. "How 'bout you, you serve?"

"No, I rode my school deferment until the lottery. I drew lucky, so I was able to stay at home and raise my family," Rory answered. "Rory O'Connor." He held out his hand. For a split second he wondered if the vet would return in kind; he was relieved when he did.

"PFC Martin Lewis," he said extending his hand. "And, no, my middle name is not 'And,' although that might be a pretty good story to tell."

Rory chuckled. "Yeah that would be pretty funny. I'm forever mystified by what people name their kids. Seems like some of them want to see if the kid can overcome their name, like George Foreman naming all of his kids "George Foreman." I mean, they're probably not ever going to have to work a day in their life, but still. . . ."

"Yeah, I knew an ol' boy named Ben Dover," offered the vet, "and he was getting ripped from everybody all of the time."

"Was this in Nam?" Rory asked.

"Yeah, he took a round right between the eyes at Khe Sanh. The big joke was that Ben Dover forgot to keep his head down. You know, to bend over."

Noticing the vet's glass was empty, Rory held up two fingers indicating a new beer for PFC Lewis and his friend. Rory's glass was still full.

"'Preciate it," the vet said as he raised his glass. "And to what do we owe the honor of your presence at our little home away from home?"

"Oh, I'm just kind of on a fact-finding mission," Rory explained. "I heard that this was where Bukowski used to come, and I wondered if he left any magic behind him."

"You a writer?"

"I don't really know how to answer that," Rory said. "I make my living from my books, but I don't really feel like a writer. Not a writer like Bukowski."

"'Buttkowski,' I called him. Never bought a round ever. Not even after he made it big. He'd just sit on that stool at the end of the bar, scribbling in his little spiral notebook until closing time or he fell off the stool, whichever came first. Stingiest son of a gun I ever met. Be glad you're not like him." Purged of his Bukowski feelings, PFC Lewis banged his empty glass down on the bar, forcing Rory to order another round.

"So, you actually knew him?" Rory queried.

"Knew him? Like as not it was me draggin' him back to his place every night. He was a strange duck, but I've met stranger. What's your interest?" the PFC squinted his sniper eye at Rory, trying to read him.

"To be painfully honest, I've come to a crossroads in my career. I can't write the drivel I've been writing anymore. I want to be like Bukowski and write about what interests me. I don't care if anyone else likes it, if it sells or doesn't. I just want to be free to write on my own terms."

The vet turned his head sideways to look at Rory from a different vantage. "It's still a free country, ain't it? I mean, that's what me and Willy and a few hundred thousand other grunts were fighting for, so a draft dodger could write what he wanted to write." Quickly recovering his sense of time and space, and fearing the loss of a benefactor, he said quickly, "Not that there's anything wrong with dodging the draft. Wish I'd been more successful at it myself."

Rather than being offended, Rory was now more interested in the barfly than before. "You tried to avoid the draft?"

"Absolutely, most certainly," PFC Lewis answered, tapping his empty glass with his middle finger. "I changed majors three times to try to maintain my student deferment. Like they say, 'All good things must end.' I was going to have to graduate in something. I knew the military industrial complex was waiting for me, so I figured I'd outsmart them and join the Navy. Turns out the Navy has this special branch for people they feel like are better suited for work on land."

"Yeah?"

"Yeah. That's how I wound up in the Marines," he said as he took a long pull from his fresh beer. "I thought, 'They're sending everybody to Vietnam. Where's the safest place to be?' I figured a ship out in the ocean, even if the ship was just off the coast. I never figured the services could trade enlistees like trading cards. I report to the MEPS, take some tests, and find out I'm best suited for the Marines. The next thing I know, I'm off to Parris Island, South Carolina. They don't even send me to Pendleton, here in California. They send me all the way to a mosquito-infested swamp in the heart of Bubba country."

Sensing the sun setting through the dinge-covered windows, Rory glanced at his watch. "I've got to go," he declared as he stood up. "Look, I'm fascinated by your story, and I'd like to hear more. Will you be here tomorrow?"

"I can usually be counted on to frequent this establishment from the hours of opening to closing unless my manager has a gig for me performing for the King and Queen of England." He grinned widely in case Rory didn't realize he was joking. "Yeah, I'll be here."

"Great," Rory replied. "I'll see you about the same time tomorrow, that is if the royal family doesn't call."

Rory headed home at a faster pace than usual. Primarily his haste was to beat sundown; he didn't like to drive at night, particularly on the mountainous road leading to his house. When he opened the garage door, he could see that his wife had returned from her quest looting and pillaging the shops of Los Angeles. His bride was in the kitchen grilling assorted vegetables and mushrooms on the JennAir grill. "Supper in ten," she called as she saw her husband slide behind her and down the stairs to his study.

Rory flipped on his computer and fired up his word processor. Normally his order of operation was to deal with emails before attempting anything else, but not right now. He stared at the blank page and began typing, *The quick brown fox jumped over the foxhole, much to the amazement of the young Marine recruit hiding within. The recruit had just that second raised his head to swat the mosquito biting him on the neck when the fox had gone aerial above him. Had the mosquito not been such a vicious bloodsucker, the recruit might have missed the vixen.* Rory leaned back in his overpriced chair, with a grin from ear to ear. The grin hadn't diminished one centimeter when he answered the call of "Supper!" from the top of the stairs.

"You look like you've had a good day," Trudy commented as she heaped onto his plate the results of her Cooking the Mediterranean Way course taken in Tuscany.

"Yeah, looks like I can say the same about you," he said, and nodded toward the designer shopping bags lining the wall.

"I did OK," Trudy answered tentatively, probably suspecting that Rory was about to deliver a lecture on moderation. Looking up from her plate of pasta primavera, she was pleasantly surprised to see her husband still grinning from ear to ear. "What's got you looking like the cat that ate the canary?"

"Well, I discovered that I can still write, and that's pretty, pretty huge," he said as he reached for another helping of the main course. "I might have tapped into a resource that will be as lucrative as Fiona, but not as soul crushing."

"Tell me more." Trudy broke off another chunk of the pumpernickel loaf to dip in her plate of olive oil and balsamic vinegar.

"I don't want to jinx it by saying too much," Rory said, grabbing the last of the bread. "It's just in the genesis. It's going to require a lot of research, and I'm going to have to go into town to do it. But-"

"But you think you might be on to something?" Trudy finished her husband's sentence.

"Yeah, I just might be."

~ ~ ~

True to his word, PFC Lewis reported for duty at the He's Not Here lounge every day. Rory brought his recorder and a notepad to document the tales of modern warfare from the loquacious ex-marine. As long as the beers kept coming, the ex-jarhead regaled Rory with tales from the sublime to the astounding. To his amazement, Rory found that he was almost as interested in the training and indoctrination process as he was to hear about how the training was implemented. Rory was fascinated by the psychology of taking "normal," "healthy" individuals and turning them into "lean, mean killing machines."

Eventually the sessions moved to the corner booth where the vet's buddy sat silently taking it all in. Glasses of beer were replaced by pitchers in the interest of efficiency. The barkeep was at the ready when he saw the last glass being poured from the pitcher. Rory worried that the greasy hamburger and fries he ordered for lunch each day were undoing all the good work that Trudy's Mediterranean diet was trying to accomplish. He rationalized that he couldn't afford to break the flow of the vet's stories. PFC Lewis had a million of them, and Rory hoped to hear them all.

After an exhausting day of hearing the insider details of the Battle of Khe Sanh, Rory drove home at a rapid clip. A fire inside him needed to be quelched, and Rory knew the only way to douse it was to put it on paper. Explaining his plan to his wife as he gathered up a basket of snacks, he beelined to his computer and continued to tell the story of the marine startled by the fox. He wrote through the night. At ten the next morning the alarm on his phone sounded. Rory called the bar and told the barkeep to provide his friends with libations and food until he returned. "Keep them happy," Rory advised.

Destined to Die was written over the next week. Only bathroom breaks and the occasional sit-down meal interrupted his process. The first in the Fortune's Soldier series had been written. He sent the manuscript to his publisher, where it was promptly rejected. Rory wasn't surprised and was glad to have the formality of giving his publisher the right of first refusal out of the way. Surveying his options, Rory came upon a unique solution available only to monied people. Knowing there was a stigma attached to self-publishing, he looked for a publisher that might need a cash infusion. He quickly found that the one constant among publishers was that *all* of them needed a cash infusion. He chose a publisher that had been very successful publishing Westerns in the '50s and '60s.

Durango Press was located on Drexel Avenue between Crescent Heights Boulevard and La Brea Park. It was close enough to Television City to walk home for lunch, if writers in the early days of television had been allowed a lunch break. Rory arrived at the pink stucco building promptly at noon and pressed the For Service button. Looking at the camera above the door he smiled and said, "I'm Rory O'Connor, and I have an appointment with Mr. Woods." The door buzzed back, and Rory could hear the lock being released.

He entered what was once an office. Now it was a desk, a few chairs, and piles and piles of what were most likely manuscripts. Somewhat disarmed at seeing the hopes and dreams of fellow writers stacked about the place like cordwood, Rory was tempted to turn tail and run away. Fortunately, his gaze went to the wall where he saw posters of some of the great early TV Westerns. *The Big Valley*, *Bonanza*, *Gunsmoke*, *Rawhide*, *The Virginian*, and *Wagon Train* were all displayed proudly. The poster that drew his attention the most, though, was from *The Treasure of the Sierra Madre*.

"Thank God the old man was there to temper John, or we would have all killed him," the voice came from a smallish man who could have played Walter Huston's double in the movie. "I'm Ed Woods. And, no, not Ed Wood. *Ed Woods.*"

The elder gentleman stuck out his hand, and Rory was impressed by its calluses. "You must still be riding a bit," Rory remarked.

"I like to keep my hand in," the elder replied. "There is something about the outside of a horse that is good for the inside of a man."

Rory remembered the phrase from a Disney cartoon where Goofy was learning to ride. He was sure the old man wasn't quoting Goofy.

"Follow me," Ed said, and led Rory upstairs to a tea set on the coffee table of what Rory presumed was Ed's living room. Again, he was struck by the wall art. Just about every cowboy Rory could remember was pictured on the walls, shaking hands or hugging a much more vibrant version of his host.

"I'm going to let you gawk for about five more minutes, and then we've got to get down to business. I've got a personal masseuse coming in an hour, and I don't like to be distracted by anything while she's here."

"Oh, OK, sorry," Rory said. "I'm just so much in awe of what you've done."

"Did," corrected the old man. "I've not had a hit book or screenplay in forty years. Which makes me even more curious why you dug me up. You don't need me. I hear you're filthy rich from your own books."

"True," Rory began, "but is that enough?"

For the next forty minutes he explained his writer's block, his unhappiness, and the serendipitous moment when he found the cure for both. The old man listened without comment and gave a slight nod at some of the more salient moments of Rory's story. When he finished, he looked at Ed for a response.

"And you need me how?" Ed asked.

"I need an established publisher. I need a man with contacts, a man who knows the ropes of this eentertainment business, and a man who isn't afraid to tell stories that are raw and contain the best and worst of humanity." Rory took a breath. "I'm writing stories about modern-day warriors, not cowboys, but something more. I guess if we equate the evolution of the warriors from the *Seven Samurai* into the gunslingers of *The Magnificent Seven*, we can make a comparison, but these men are so much more."

"And?"

"And I'm willing to give you five hundred thousand to be your silent partner," Rory answered. "I'll pay for you to staff the office. Readers, editors, designers—whatever you say we need. What I require of you is your good name and help with getting the stories in the right places."

"And the back end?" the old man inquired with a grin.

"Same deal. It's fifty-fifty after the expenses are covered."

The old man stuck out his hand. "Used to be a handshake was all you needed. Man's only as good as his word, you know?"

Rory stuck out his hand and shook his partner's vigorously. "True, true. I'll have my lawyer draw up the papers and send them to your lawyer, OK?"

"Sounds fine. What are we going to call this new venture?" Ed asked.

"Durango Press, of course," Rory answered. "Durango was where *The Treasure of the Sierra Madre* was filmed, right?"

"Yep, as miserable a spot as you can imagine. And when you add John Huston to it, well, it was like hell on earth." Ed chuckled. "I'm enjoying this trip down memory lane, but I have that prior engagement, you know?"

"Sure, sure, I'll be in touch," Rory said as he heard the buzzer of the front door sound. He passed a woman who could have been Fay Wray's double on his way out the door. Pulling his car into the street, he couldn't decide whether to go home or celebrate with his new buddies at the He's Not Here. The impossibility of making a turn across oncoming traffic made the decision for him. He went home.

The lawyers agreed on terms, the participants signed the contract, and the manuscript for *Destined to Die* arrived at the offices of Durango Press by courier the next day. Over the course of a hectic thirty days, the editing, formatting, and cover design for the book were completed. Ed Woods leaned on the influential people he knew who were "still above ground" to create a stir about the new book, which rocketed to number one in sales on Amazon in the category Vietnam War History. Shortly after the book hit the *New York Times* bestseller list it was announced that a major studio had picked up the option to make the book into a film.

Rory slid into the corner booth of the He's Not Here bar and joined the men who were already half a pitcher of beer ahead of him.

"Who'd you like to play you in the movie?" he asked PFC Lewis.

"Huh?" was the reply.

"I'm thinking that it's got to be a fresh face, somebody that doesn't have a rom-com or some other silly something in his credits to confuse the audience. We want this guy to pop onto the screen and just appear to be hard-core from the get-go," Rory said as he poured the last of the pitcher into his glass. "We want him to be identified with this role so that when we make the second movie and the third the audience will know exactly what to expect."

"You really think they're going to make a movie about these stories I've been telling you?" the vet asked.

"I'm betting the house on it," Rory answered. "And when we get done with Vietnam, we'll take our hero to other areas of conflict. That's where you'll lend your experience." He nodded to the younger veteran. "I see our hero potentially fighting under different flags but always on the right side, if you know what I mean."

The usually reticent younger vet, who Rory learned had attained the rank of corporal, CPL Willy Sutton, chose to speak at that moment. "Free beer and lunch and all that is fine, but it seems to me like there's something more here. These are our stories, our experiences, and it looks to me like you're making bank on them. Why shouldn't we find another writer fella and tell him our stories? Maybe there's a better deal in here somewhere."

Serendipity chose to bring the bartender with a fresh pitcher of beer at just that moment. Rory held up his hand to the bartender, halting his progress. He started to slide from the booth. "Maybe you're right. Maybe somebody else is better suited to translate your stories for you. You guys have been forced into the most horrible situations by our country against your will. I will not make a bad situation worse. I will just leave this with Martin and be on my way."

Rory handed Martin a check for $10,500. "This is your share of the royalties for *Destined to Die*. I had planned on two more books from you. I have no idea how many books I can get from our young friend. I had planned on using you both as technical assistants on the movie if it gets made. Willy thinks he can get a better deal. What do you think?"

"I think Willy's a damn fool is what I think," Martin said as his eyes glazed over from the numbers on the check. "I can meet you at another bar, closer to you if you like. I've got plenty of buddies from the VA that would be willing to help you with whatever excursion you want to talk about. Hell, I even know a guy that was in Grenada. That was the cluster of all clusters, and I guarantee you that story's never been told."

Rory motioned for the bartender to keep coming. "Let me think about it. I agree, there's a thousand stories out there. For some reason, this environment clicked. Who knows if another one might click as well."

"Sir, I apologize," said Willy as he stood, nearly tipping the table over in the process. "My daddy always said that my momma had dropped me too many times as a child and that was why I was so slow. He drove me to the induction center himself. Told me I was somebody else's problem now and that he hoped they could make a man out of me."

The lanky, tousled-hair veteran of too many wars stuck out his hand. "Sir, I do apologize."

Rory looked at the hand and the trembling lip of the lean, mean killing machine and grasped his hand with as strong a grip as he could. "Forgotten, water under the bridge. If you're ready to talk, we'll start recording you tomorrow, if that's OK?"

"Yes, sir, that will be OK," Willy replied.

"Good I'll see you then," Rory answered.

Rory's mind was racing as he pushed his Mustang through the canyons on the way back home. *Maybe one can gain courage by osmosis,* he thought as the speedometer climbed higher. When the speedometer hit eighty he remembered that courage should always be tempered by caution, and he allowed the Mustang to slow to fifty-five.

~ ~ ~

The Fortune's Soldier series included two more works from the Vietnam era, *Drive On By* and *It Don't Mean Nothin'*. Rory painfully pulled six books from the various 'Stans that Willy had served in. The last one, *Thank You for Your Service*, barely created a blip on the *New York Times* charts. The first two 'Stan books were offered movie deals based off the success of the Vietnam books. The audience for war movies, at least recent ones, was diminishing, and no more movie deals were offered.

Confident that he had done his part in returning a vet to society, Rory closed his tab at the He's Not Here. Martin and Willy had worked as technical assistants on several movies after their introduction by Rory to the right people. If they kept their noses clean, they would be set for life. Rory was proud to have brought their stories to life, but more importantly, he was elated at burying Hillary Bruchette Adams. Her ghost did appear occasionally, but Rory was able to exorcise her with minimal effort.

Ed Woods, cowboy, writer, and publisher, handed over the reins to Durango Press to Rory by expiring. Rory paid his respects to the man who had given him a new lease on life by commissioning a

Frederic Remington–like sculpture to mark the old cowboy's grave. While Ed was alive, everything had gotten done effortlessly it seemed. Rory was trying to learn the ropes of the publishing world, but did not have the proficiency of the old cowboy. The ropes just seemed to get more tangled each day.

Meanwhile, at a new mansion overlooking the San Fernando Valley, the quick brown fox jumped over the lazy dog all the way down the page and beyond.

PROPERTY OVER LIFE

Trooper Alex Murtaugh approached the garage of the Pensacola Florida Highway Patrol station with a joy that was usually reserved for his birthday or Christmas. Today was the day, he hoped. Being the lowest in seniority meant that he was always last in the unit to receive any upgrades or new equipment. He had waited patiently for this day for over six months. The threatened budget cuts from the new governor had placed his rise in status in jeopardy. Backroom pressure from one group or another had finally resulted in the governor releasing the funds necessary to implement the program. The pressure had come from the news media as well. No fiscally conservative Republican wanted to be associated with "defunding the police" no matter the extravagance. A true conservative would have argued what an extravagance the upgrade was.

"A-Man," the mechanic known as Shorty called to the trooper as he entered the garage. "Coming to check up on your new whip?"

Alex looked up at the six-foot, seven-inch giant and nodded in agreement. "Yep, this one mine?"

"Indeed, it is," Shorty replied with a big grin. "I was just trying to decide whether to set the governor at seventy or seventy-five. I can't let you young pups get into too much mischief."

As Alex watched the mechanic maneuver the wrenches in an engine compartment filled with the most horsepower available, he was awestruck. He wondered how a man so physically unsuited for a job could be doing what he did. The mechanic's hands were as big as hams, and there was virtually no space to maneuver. Everything had to be done by extensions attached to wrenches, sockets, or drivers to adjust the components necessary to keep the car in peak condition.

"You know at some point you're going to outgrow your profession," Alex offered.

Shorty laughed. "I did that when I was sixteen. Of course, back then I could get my whole arm down in the engine compartment. There used to be so much more car and so much less engine. Shoot, I used to be able to undo the oil filter from up top, with just one hand. Not anymore. Now you have to get underneath and use a special tool, and God help you if you don't catch all that oil. The EPA keeps track of every drop, somehow."

Finished under the hood, Shorty moved to the driver compartment. There he nimbly moved his fingers over the screen of the Motopower diagnostic tool and checked all the settings.

"All right, young man," he said as he stood to his full height. "Here's your lecture. This is a Dodge Charger Pursuit model. It has a 5.7L Hemi V8 engine and can reach sixty miles per hour from a standing start in 6.4 seconds, which is kind of slow compared to some of the cars you might get entangled with. Of course, it's carrying a few hundred pounds of equipment that a Porsche or Corvette won't be draggin' around. Where you have the advantage is at the top end. Out of the box it will do one fifty-five, but I am mandated to set the top speed to one thirty. Because of my advanced years I occasionally forget to set the governor correctly, and some units have gone into the field with factory settings. Who knows, maybe this one."

At this point, he held out the keys to the young trooper, but then pulled them back. "I just want you to remember that this car won't stop at speed as quickly as you or I would like. I've beefed up the brakes and the suspension, but it is no match for a sports car or motorcycle. It's great in a straight line. If someone leaves the interstate, let the locals handle it or let 'em go and catch them another day. Got it?"

"Sure," Alex answered as he reached for the keys of the bumblebee-wrapped patrol car. "Can we go for a spin?"

"That's why I'm here," Shorty replied. "Just let me wash my hands. I don't want to gum up your new pretty."

Before taking to the highway, Alex had to adjust the seat from Shorty's reach to his own. At five feet, nine inches, Alex was nearly a foot shorter than the mechanic. Seat and mirrors adjusted, the lawmen were ready to go. The pair left the garage of Troop A and headed north on Highway 29 to the I-10 interchange. As Alex drove, Shorty pointed out buttons and features of the new cruiser. They tested the zero-to-sixty standard on the ramp to I-10 westbound. Even discounting the fact that the ramp was slightly inclined, Alex was not impressed. Once they were clear of Pensacola traffic, they were able to open up the cruiser a bit. They crossed into Alabama at

130 miles per hour. Alex was happy to confirm that he still had more pedal under his right foot. Shorty must have "forgotten" to set the governor to the state patrol standard. They exited at the first exit and returned to the garage at the posted speed limit. Alex was tingling all over.

He was still smiling when he brought the cruiser home. State troopers were allowed personal use of the patrol cars in Florida, and Alex felt it was a necessary perk to supplement his salary. Truth was, he would have been a trooper for free if he could figure out how to feed his family and pay his bills. He loved the work, he loved the uniform, and now he loved his new car. Some troopers referred to their cars as "the other woman" because they spent more time with their cars than they did with their actual wives.

Bea waved to him from the front door of the two-bedroom stucco house they rented from Bea's uncle. Alex reciprocated the wave by putting the car in neutral and flooring the engine, which created a sound blast that shook windows in his neighbors' houses. The sound brought his kids to the door to join their mother.

"Y'all wanna go for a ride?" Alex yelled from the street.

The young family scurried to the car and piled in. Alex had a moment of anxiety while seat belting his children into the back seat without approved car seats, but it passed. The fact that his children were behind a cage designed to keep suspects at bay reassured him in a way. He knew in a crash they would in all likelihood be protected by the cage, like a roll bar in a race car.

"It's so pretty and smells brand new." Bea pulled her seat belt across her chest. "Look at the computer. It's twice as big as your old one." She reached to touch the screen, but Alex grabbed her hand before she could touch the display.

"It's all touchscreen now," he said, and released her hand. "We don't have to type on a keyboard like before. We can just touch the screen and it'll work."

"Cool," said Bea. "Is it fast?"

"It'll run like a scalded dog," Alex replied as he pulled from the curb, and the ear-to-ear grin returned to his face.

The family didn't get an example of how fast a scalded dog could run on that trip. They observed the speed limit to and from the Baskin-Robbins. The children's hands and faces were washed meticulously before the return trip home. Ants in a vehicle were one of the signs that a trooper was abusing the privilege of the loaner car. Alex couldn't bear the thought of having his "baby" taken away from him.

He parked that night under the streetlight as he had for the four years of his service with the patrol. He hoped that the bright light would discourage any miscreants who saw a patrol car as an opportunity for mischief. On a more primal level, he wanted as much light as possible to aim his service revolver should the need arise. Alex realized it was just a car and that a life was more valuable, but there was something wrong with someone who attacked a police car. Society had slipped into decay, Alex feared, and the lack of respect for the symbols of order was just the tip of the iceberg.

~ ~ ~

"A-Man, what's shakin'?" asked the trooper attempting to bench press 315 pounds. "How about a spot?"

"Sure, sure," Alex said, and threw his sweat towel to the wall. "Going for a PR, are we?"

"I don't know what 'we' are doing today," Trooper Gene Baker answered. "But I feel like today's the day."

With two deep breaths, he pulled the weight from the rack. He slowed the weight's progress to his chest just enough to keep it from breaking his sternum. Once the bar touched his chest, the trooper bounced the weight by heaving his hips. The motion sent the weight back toward the rack. With a primitive scream, he completed the lift and returned the weight safely to the rack. Alex didn't know whether to be more concerned about the blood-red color of the trooper's face or the enlarged carotid arteries on either side of his neck.

"You did it," Alex exclaimed as he extended his fist for a congratulatory fist bump.

"Yeah." Trooper Baker slowly acknowledged the fist bump. "Well, that's it for me today. Can I spot you before I go?"

"No, thanks, today's cardio for me," Alex said as he grabbed his towel and turned toward the treadmills that lined the wall.

"Yeah, well, like I always say, if I have to run a perp down, it's going to be with a car. I ain't gettin' in a footrace with one of these porch monkeys," the beefy trooper responded. "If just one of us is coming home for supper, it's going to be me." He took his towel and wiped off the bench and the bar. "You're my witness, I got three wheels today. Back me up if I call on you."

"Always. You know I've got your back," Alex said as he set the treadmill for five miles an hour and pressed the Start button. "Semper fi!" he said to the back of the only other Marine Corps veteran at Troop A. His salutation was ignored.

The thirty-minute jog on the treadmill helped Alex attain a calmer state of mind. Each shift, he arrived at the station completely amped, ready for anything. Most mornings he was awake before the clock sounded. He would literally spring out of bed ready to go to work catching bad guys. He loved his job, almost as much as he loved his car and his family.

Most days were long slogs of nothingness. No bank robberies, no murders, no stolen cars fleeing capture, just days driving below the speed limit waiting for something to happen. It was those moments when something did happen that Alex and the rest of the patrol lived for. Those moments when the lawmen could display their skills and help return society back to the order it so desperately needed.

It was on one of the more boring shifts when Alex got to take his new baby for a run. Alex had been posted in the median just on the downside of a rise on I-10 westbound when his radar started blipping furiously. The digital response blinked 88 MPH on the radar gun. The blue blur flashed by, and Alex locked onto his target. Lights and sirens engaged, Alex slipped into the left-hand lane of the interstate, employing his zero-to-sixty speed to merge into traffic.

As the cars ahead of him slid to the middle lane, Alex spied his target just ahead. He pulled up behind the car and waited for the driver to understand Alex's "Yes, I'm here for you." The driver seemed to be unaware, and Alex pulled up close enough to recognize the Toyota symbol on the trunk. He started his siren into the *whoop whoop* function, which guaranteed even the most distracted driver would notice the patrol car. The speeder appeared to notice and drifted his car toward the shoulder.

Assuming the driver was going to comply, Alex started to relay the particulars to dispatch. The second he reached for the microphone, the Toyota sped up as if shot from a cannon. Surprised, Alex dropped the mike. Simultaneously, he dropped the hammer on the Dodge Charger Pursuit cruiser. Speeds of 100, 120, 130 were reached in seconds. Alex would pull closer, and the Toyota would find another gear, another ten horsepower or some mechanical wizardry that would keep the trooper at bay.

The Alabama line loomed closer, and Alex knew his chance of bringing the speeder to justice was drawing nigh. With his foot fully pressed on the accelerator, he unleashed the full fury of the Dodge's Hemi engine. As the speedometer hit 155 and bounced, the Toyota pulled away again and crossed into Alabama. Alex let off the accelerator and left the freeway at the first exit to return home. For the first time as a trooper, he was going home with his tail between his legs.

Rather than go back to his post, Alex asked for permission to go 10-7. He returned to the garage and drove his cruiser into an empty bay.

"A-Man, what's up?" Shorty called from the picnic table sitting in front of the office.

"I need you to pull my dashcam and see if we can figure out what just happened," Alex said with frustration tainting his voice. "I just got my butt handed to me by a Toyota, and I can't tell you if the driver was white or black or pink, young or old, male or female. I couldn't get close enough to see who was driving. Whoever he was, or she was, is a driver, and whatever it is that they're driving is some sort of pocket rocket that I didn't know existed."

Alex was now standing as close to face-to-face as the disparity in their heights would allow. "I thought with this new car I was supposed to be the king of the road, and right now I feel like a princess."

The giant reached his hands out and placed them on the trooper's shoulders. "Now, now, let's not get our underwear all in a bunch. Go get yourself a pop, and Uncle Shorty will have a look-see at what's going on."

Alex did as instructed and waited for Shorty to return with the dashcam.

"Let's have a look at this thing," the mechanic said as he opened the door to the office. They connected the camera to a large monitor, and the lights were turned off. The playback of what Alex felt was his most humiliating career moment was before them.

"Hmmm," Shorty said. "I think I have identified the source of your discomfort. That's not just a Toyota. That's a Toyota MK4. They eat 'vettes for breakfast."

He started the playback again and said, "They're pretty rare. It might not be too hard finding this one. I see he has cleverly spread mud across his tag so we can't read his numbers. We can tell it's an Alabama tag, 'cause the stars, like their teeth, come out at night." Shorty pointed to the familiar logo on the Alabama tag, "Stars Fell on Alabama."

Shorty flipped the light back on. "Here's the thing. These things come from the factory governed at a hundred sixty miles per hour. Your car, ungoverned, tops out at one fifty-five. If they took the governor off this car, which it appears that they have, that baby might roll to two hundred or beyond. That's not a chase you want to be in. It's easier just to figure out who this dude is and go wake him up at the crack of dawn. You hear me?"

"I hear you," Alex answered. "But doesn't that kind of miss the point? If the police can't catch the bad guys, they'll just go on doing what they want to."

"You ain't hearing me," Shorty said sternly. "He got away this time. That doesn't mean he's going to stay uncaught. That's a fairly expensive piece of machinery. It takes resources to keep them up. It takes skill to keep them between the ditches. I wouldn't be surprised if the driver wasn't involved in racing—NASCAR or Formula One. He didn't seem to be too concerned when you pulled up on his bumper. It was like he'd been in that position before."

Shorty carried the dashcam over to his computer. "I'm going to make a copy of this for our files. You want a copy?"

"I certainly do. I want to get started on identifying this clown right away," Alex answered. "Maybe you're right. Giving him an early morning wake-up call might just be the ticket. The ticket, get it?"

"Now you're thinking with your head." Shorty chuckled and then turned serious again. "The important thing is that at the end of the day everybody makes it home safe. You, the perp, and John Q. Public. There's nothing as precious as a human life. Our motto says it all: 'Courtesy, service, protection.' Although, to tell the truth, I'd put protection first. I guess our idiot governor felt like he needed to improve on 'Protect and serve.'"

Finished with the copies, Shorty started back into the garage to replace the dash cam. "How'd she do other than not being rocket powered?" he asked as he sat in the driver's seat.

"Fine. The front end got a little light when I hit top end, but other than that, I felt like she could have done more," Alex critiqued.

"Yeah, well, that ain't goin' to happen." Shorty unfolded from the front seat. "Now go do your homework, and let's get speed racer off of the road the safe way."

"Roger that."

~ ~ ~

Alex poured over the internet that night and read every article he could find on the MK4. He was tempted to read an article about the car to his four-year-old son for his bedtime story but opted for a Thomas the Train book instead. With the children down, he spent the rest of the evening reading specifications of the car.

He located the dealerships authorized to service the cars and used the Texas Department of Motor Vehicles list to identify all the registered owners of MK4s in the US. He knew it wasn't a comprehensive list. There were gray-market and black-market cars being brought in and traded all the time, but he needed a start.

The young trooper also needed a channel for his energy. The thrill of driving 155 miles per hour in a high-speed chase didn't just dissipate when the chase was over. He was still twitchy when Bea went to bed.

The morning found Alex full of his usual vigor. He was ready to hit the streets with his newfound knowledge when Bea and the kids came into the kitchen-dining room. Kisses and hugs all around, and he was out the door to conquer the highways and byways of the Florida thoroughfares.

Around midday, Alex was posted at the same rise in the median at mile marker 13 as his previous encounter with the MK4. As he reached for the microphone to request a 10-7 for lunch, a green blur flashed by the corner of his eye.

The radar gun blinked 92 MPH as Alex floored the patrol car into action. The green blur was a motorcycle, later identified as a Kawasaki Ninja. The Ninja was stealthily winding its way through traffic, occasionally passing two cars at once by driving between them. The startled drivers yielded to Alex's sirens and flashing lights. The cruiser under full throttle caught up to the Ninja quickly.

Pulling to within fifty feet of the motorcycle, Alex went to his speaker to tell the motorist to pull over. The motorcyclist responded by raising his left land in an obscene gesture of defiance. The Ninja's driver cranked his right hand on the throttle while attempting to coordinate his left hand with the clutch and negotiating the gear shift with his left foot. Something went wrong, and the motorcycle lost momentum instantly. Alex attempted to brake and veer at the same time. The maneuver resulted in the patrol car clipping the Kawasaki's rear tire with the rear of his cruiser. The impact sent the motorcycle and rider airborne.

The sound of horns and screeching brakes filled the air along with the sound of the motorcycle grinding its way to a stop. The motorcycle lay on its side in the grass off the shoulder of the highway. The rider lay just inside the right-hand lane. He was motionless. Alex quickly turned his car sideways in the lane to protect the speeder from oncoming traffic. A few motorists had gotten out of their cars to lend assistance with traffic control. Alex ran to the bleeding body.

The rider was dressed in typical Florida high-speed motorcycle gear. Flip flops, jean shorts, tank top, and no helmet. Alex called for an ambulance. A check of the rider's pulse confirmed his worst fears. Thirteen minutes later the EMTS verified Alex's diagnosis.

The trooper was taken back to the station by his sergeant. The motorcyclist was taken to the morgue. Alex gave his statement and counted on the dashcam to confirm his version of the details. He was given three days' suspension while the investigators sorted through the facts. Like a caged animal, he paced back and forth in his two-bedroom home, snapping at anything that came near. Finally, the call came, and he was placed back on active duty.

~ ~ ~

His new post, if it could be called a post, was traffic control for a bridge that was being repaired. The last hurricane had done extensive damage to the highways and bridges in the area. Most of the construction sites were outside of the local police jurisdiction. It came to the highway patrol to maintain a presence at these spots to provide a safe environment for the repair crews.

Alex felt fortunate that he had been allowed to keep his cruiser for the new assignment. Parking on the side of the road with lights flashing was a waste of horsepower and manpower. *But you do what you gotta' do*, he thought.

For eight hours a day the trooper waved the procession of cars away from workers. He had been fortunate not to draw the night shift for the punishment that was not a punishment but a "disciplining." At least he didn't have to suffer the indignity of missing supper and bedtime with his kids because he had committed a traffic faux pas.

Waxing philosophical, Alex approached his time amongst the big orange barrels as a time to sharpen his mental game. He had the driving skills; there was no doubt about that. *I just need to get my mental game in better shape*, he concluded. Replaying the accident over and over, he surmised that had he been more to the side of the motorcycle he likely would have missed the rider. Perhaps not pulling so close to the Ninja's brake light and blasting "Get over!" through the speakers might have changed the outcome. Alex wasn't sure what caused the rider to bungle shifting his gears; he just wanted to be taken out of the equation.

It was during one of these reveries that the call came over the radio. A 10-90 emanating from the First Citizens Bank less than two miles away. Unsure of his duties in that particular situation, Alex radioed dispatch that he was 10-8 less than two miles away from the bank. Dispatch answered quickly: "Stand down. We are advised that the Escambia sheriff's department is in pursuit."

Just under the dispatcher's voice, Alex could hear the wail of sirens coming his way. Leading the tan and brown sheriff's car was a blue Toyota MK4. Without replying to dispatch, Alex threw his car into gear and got in line behind the sheriff's car. The construction workers were on their own.

Based off his prior experience, Alex knew the suspect would be attempting to get to I-10, where his superior enginery would carry him to the safety of the state line. Alex felt like his only hope of preventing an escape was to get in front of the suspect and somehow slow the suspect's progress. He caught the sheriff's cruiser within a mile and whipped into the oncoming lane to pass the constable. Alex pulled right up behind the MK4. The driver of the Toyota was a true professional. He used the oncoming lane, the shoulder, and turns onto side roads at breakneck speeds to try to lose the trooper. Alex was like a dog with a bone, though; he was not going to let go.

He tried to update dispatch with their location and direction as best he could. It was Alex's tertiary plan that he would drive the fleeing suspect into the waiting arms of his patrol brothers. Plan B would be a pit maneuver to incapacitate the accused. Frustrated by every stratagem of the MK4, Alex could see that he was not dictating the terms of the race.

At one point the trooper thought he had the suspect trapped on a street with no outlet. Suddenly the suspect stopped, U-turned, and went back in the direction that they had come from at his "zero to sixty in 4.4 seconds" speed. Alex struggled to get the Charger turned around and headed in the right direction while maintaining visual contact with the suspect. He failed.

About to resign from the race, he glimpsed a blur of blue down a side road. *He'll always be heading toward the interstate. He needs the open road to take advantage of his superior car.*

Alex caught up to the suspect at the confluence of roads on the outskirts of a shopping mall. The road had widened to four lanes, and the interstate was less than a mile away. He knew from the radio chatter that the patrol had not had time to block the entrance ramp. Whipping into oncoming traffic, Alex attempted to get ahead of the fleeing suspect. Looking to his right at the MK4, Alex didn't see the minivan carrying the family of five pulling out from the Kentucky Fried Chicken. He struck the minivan just at the passenger-side wheel well, catapulting it upside down into the median.

Sharon Goudchaux, age twenty-eight, died instantly from the blow. The sideways force had snapped her neck. Her husband, Tommy, age twenty-seven, drowned in the standing water in the median ditch. His body was pinned in by the airbag, which allowed just enough space around him to let water enter his lungs. The minivan stood on its nose in the ditch for over forty-five minutes while desperate citizens tried to free the three children from their car seats in the back. Attempts to push the van back to level ground were to no avail. The force of the blow had firmly planted the minivan so solidly in the muddy ditch that it required a tow truck to free it.

The fleeing suspect made it to the safety of the interstate and presumably to the safety of his lair.

Alex was placed on desk detail while the investigation of the accident was underway. The local newspapers attempted to keep the story on the front page for as long as they could, hoping to highlight the dangers to the public of high-speed police chases. The papers had dug deep enough into the story to unearth the fact that Alex and Sharon, the victim, had dated in high school. Alex could find no peace in anything he did.

Finally, he was absolved of all wrongdoing in the incident and cleared for active duty. Entering the garage for the first time since the accident, he tried to project the confidence, the swagger he had once had.

"How's it going, Killer?" The giant standing beside the Coke machine confronted him. "Buy you a pop?"

"Uh, no, no thanks." Alex sat down at the picnic table. "Uh, I don't think you can call me that."

"I think I can call you whatever I dang well please," Shorty replied as he sat down. "And if you or anyone complains, well, they can just kiss my backside, if they can jump up that high."

The mechanic squeezed onto the bench of the picnic table and finished half the bottle of Coke in one swallow. Belching loudly, he clasped both hands around the bottle and stared intently into the eyes of the young patrolman. "Five thousand eight hundred and fifty dollars is what he got. That's less than three thousand dollars per life. Three orphans that will never have the chance at a normal life, all because you couldn't let it go."

Shorty finished the bottle and got up from the table. Placing the empty in the rack, he turned back to the patrolman, who was now crying into his hands. "I tell all of you guys the same thing: never place the value of property over the value of a life. One can be replaced, the other can't. Now you know. Will it make a difference?"

"Yes," Alex replied as he sobbed. "Yes!"

And, at that moment, he meant it.

RENAL FAILURE

State Senator Darby Clements slid into the back row of the packed auditorium and surveyed the scene. In his mind it was a set right out of *Caligula*. There was no overt sexual activity, but the senator knew that each and every one of the participants in the show was just an inch away from acting out their prurient desires. He hoped that the fake beard and mustache coupled with the false eyeglasses were enough of a disguise to allow him to carry out his mission incognito. He slipped into the aisle seat of the last row as the house lights dimmed. The good senator was ready to exit quickly should there be any hint of a reason.

The ramshackle orchestra hit the opening notes of "You've Gotta Have Heart," and the dancers started filling the stage from either side. Their costumes were loosely coordinated; in fact, it was the preponderance of sequins that tied the group together. Some of the dancers wore tiaras, while others balanced pyramids of fruit on their heads. Most of the dancers were not of the svelte variety. At times their size and lack of coordination caused an unintended encounter with another dancer. The dancers tended to laugh off the blunders and continue on with their routine. After four choruses all but one of the dancers left the stage, and the spotlight centered on the soloist.

From his perch in the last row, Darby watched the heavily made-up headliner work through the set list. The routine was a trio of show tunes. While it was not Darby's favorite music, he did admit that the performer brought a lot of energy to the stage. *A lot of energy and a lot of pancake makeup,* Darby thought. He was amazed that even at his distance from the stage he could see the performer's eyelashes flutter. When the house lights dimmed for the set change, Darby stole toward the exit. *I've seen enough,* he declared mentally.

Safe within the bosom of his family, he began construction of the bill he intended to present to the state senate. When his wife tapped him on the shoulder indicating that it was bedtime, he closed his laptop reluctantly.

"I'm just not getting the flow of it," he told his wife as he got into bed. "I'm trying to quote from the Bible without being too preachy. I've got to offer an imminent threat to the community to justify what some will call an unprecedented action. It's like threading a needle."

"I'm sure you'll figure it out," Darby's wife said, and turned to face the wall. "You always do."

Darby tossed and turned fitfully until finally forcing himself to lie rigid on his back. "Still as a mouse," his mother used to say. Counting backward from one thousand eventually gained him the calm he needed to fall asleep.

His dreams were confusing. Everyday characters were placed in scenes filled with avenging angels in heavy makeup. He awoke in a cold sweat. His brain felt foggy, as though he was trying to remember something important but just couldn't grab the thread. He took longer than usual in the shower, trying to clear the cobwebs. His breakfast was getting cold when he appeared in the kitchen.

"Morning, hon," the couple called to each other simultaneously. Darby reached for the coffeepot and read the digital time displayed on the face of the Cuisinart coffee maker.

"Why did you let me sleep so late?" he accused.

"Because I knew that the only thing on your schedule for today was your physical," she answered. "Be at Dr. Smith's at the Prado Mall office at eleven. Be a good boy and do what they tell you to do, and then you're free for the rest of the day."

"Oh, OK, sorry. Thanks," he said, opening his laptop and scanning the daily news.

Each news service confirmed that the conservative movement was getting stronger and bolder across the country. Headline after headline promoted the movement's agenda and the politicians who advanced them to national prominence. Darby felt it was just a matter of time before his work would be recognized by the national party leaders as visionary. Once in the fold of the movers and shakers, Darby knew that no position would be unattainable, not even the presidency.

Darby was fifteen minutes early for his annual physical. He hated every aspect of it. The matter-of-fact attitude of the nurses and physician's assistants and the robotic motions of the doctor drove him mad. He tried to joke away his nervousness, but the jokes invariably fell flat or came across as insulting. When asked if he was getting up more often in the middle of the night to urinate, he responded, "More often than who?"

"Do you get up now more than once?" Dr. Smith asked. "Most people get up at least once."

"Yeah, I guess I've been getting up a couple of times," Darby replied. "I just figured it was because I've been drinking more flavored waters, trying to cut back on the soda pop, you know?"

"Well, that's good," the doctor said as he continued to press the flesh around Darby's ankles. "Extreme edema of the ankles," he said to his nurse, who was recording the findings in a laptop.

"How's your energy?" the doctor asked Darby. "Still playing squash every day?"

"No, I've been working on kind of a special project for the last couple of months, and I really haven't felt like playing that much. I don't know, maybe it's a seasonal thing. I think my allergies have been kicking up. I itch a lot more."

"Loss of energy and itches more," the doctor recited to the nurse.

"OK, I'm going to relieve you from what you always refer to as the 'entertainment portion of the show' for today," the doctor said as he peeled off his gloves. "We're going to take blood and urine samples, and we'll be back in touch with you as soon as we have the results. Do you have any questions for me?"

Relieved that he had dodged a bullet with regard to the prostate exam, Darby replied quickly, "No, sir, not a one."

He proudly gave three vials of 100 percent Anglo-Saxon pure blood and proceeded to the unisex bathroom to produce his urine sample. The twinge in his back was still there, but not so bad that he felt like mentioning it to the doctor. "In and out in under an hour" was his mantra when it came to medical services.

Faced with an open day, Darby surveyed the clouds and decided he had time to get in at least one round of golf before the rain hit. *What a great day*, he thought as he headed for the country club. And a great day it was as he shot just under his 10 handicap with a couple of favorable drops. His mulatto caddy could always be counted on to do the right thing for a nice tip.

After dinner, Darby holed up again in his study to try to piece together the legislation he hoped to propose that week. The Arkansas Code was open on his desk next to his family Bible. The Bible was open to Leviticus 18:22. "Thou shalt not lie with mankind, as with womankind: it is an abomination." A nagging filament of his brain tugged at the prospect that all men that dressed as women weren't homosexual, but he knew in his heart that they were. The federal government prevented him from banning gays outright, but at least he could keep them from profiting from their perversion and destroying the children of the community. Shows that featured men dressed as women might appear fun to children, and for that reason alone should be banned.

Darby pored over his "rebuttal" information. He didn't want to go into a floor debate and have his legislation shot down by some upstart Gen Zer who didn't have enough life experience to know the dangers that the homosexual lifestyle posed. Darby was aware that until the Motion Picture Production Code was passed in 1930, men had regularly portrayed women in plays and movies. In the 1500s, women were thought to be too frail and not mentally capable of performing on stage. Men routinely played the female roles to spare the fairer sex from the rigors of performance art.

The poster for *Some Like It Hot* glared back at him from his computer screen. The 1959 movie had won six Academy Award nominations for a story about two men hiding out from the mob in a girl's traveling band. *Even the most visually challenged buffoon could tell the difference between Jack Lemmon and Marilyn Monroe,* he thought as he switched on his word processor. *It was not like it is today, where men are getting operations and changing how God made them so that they can masquerade as something they're not.* He let the fire of his beliefs light up the words on the screen as he crafted his bill.

Darby was still typing furiously when his wife placed her hands on his shoulders, indicating that it was bedtime. Reluctantly he saved his work and shuffled off to bed. He had two more days before the opening session. *The soul of America depends on me getting this right.* He forced his body to be calm, and eventually, calm overtook him.

~ ~ ~

The opening-day session was unlike any other. The state had just elected the daughter of a televangelist as their new governor. Casting herself in the feminine role, the new governor promised to "sweep the state clean of any moral impurities." Christians of all denominations lined up behind the governor to rid the state of whatever abomination the followers of Jesus felt threatened the souls of their constituents the most. Seasoned veterans of congress knew just how far to push the lines of public sentiment and corporate investment.

"Thou shalt not kill" was a popular concept until put up against the untold riches placed before the congress by the gun lobbies. It was the considered opinion of the learned legislators that the first commandment needed to be tempered by the methodology of the killing. Was it tenable to leave lawful the means to murder school children in their classrooms while opposing the termination of an unviable pregnancy? *The tough decisions are left to our prophets to define the answers and our leaders to implement*, the senator from District 26 thought while he answered roll.

I am nothing. I am but an instrument, a pencil in the hands of the Lord with which He writes what He likes, Darby thought, and stood to introduce his bill to ban not only drag shows, but cross-dressing of any kind. Because of his widespread support for the governor, his bill was placed near the top of the items to be considered. There was no consideration for any kind of exception, not a male clown dressed as Clarabelle, nor a female dressed as Charlie Chaplin. The law would restrict "adult cabaret performances" in public or in the presence of children and would ban them from occurring within one thousand feet of schools, public parks, or places of worship." The bill passed sixty-seven to twenty-three, and Darby was on cloud nine.

Darby was chattering to his wife that night like a squirrel that had just found a cache of peanuts when the call came from Dr. Smith's office. They asked if he had reviewed his lab results on the patient portal yet. "I have not," Darby admitted.

"Dr. Smith would like to schedule you for an appointment as soon as possible," the voice replied.

"But, I was just there," Darby offered. "Can't it wait? I'm very busy right now."

"Please review your lab results on our patient portal. There are some concerning levels. Please make an appointment as soon as possible. You can do it right there on the portal."

Darby entered his information into the patient portal and printed out the results of his labs. He scanned through the myriad of assorted findings. They all appeared to be "within normal range." All except the results for serum creatinine and blood urea nitrogen. Both were well above the acceptable values. Discouraged that his checkup was not perfect, he signed out of the program without making an appointment. Darby employed his talents as a Google detective and researched all that he could about his report. After an hour the Google detective switched hats and became a Google doctor. Darby signed back on to the patient portal and made an appointment.

The appointment was as jovial as ever, with Darby teasing the nurse about having to weigh in again so close to his last physical. To his surprise, Darby was three pounds lighter than his weight at his previous physical. Even more surprising, he was asked to undress and don the revealing gown.

"Hmmm," began Dr. Smith as he read the chart. "Darby, how do you feel?"

"OK, I guess," Darby said. "Maybe a little blasé. I've been working really hard with the new session opening up. I'm probably not sleeping as much or as well as usual."

"Hmmm, I'd like for you to roll over on your stomach," the doctor requested.

Darby rolled over onto his stomach, conscious that he was exposing his backside to the nurse and physician's assistant. The doctor slowly touched his ankles and then his calves. He lightly touched the small of Darby's back with his thumbs on either side of the senator's spine. The touch caused Darby to wince and inhale sharply.

"Sorry," the doctor responded. "You can sit up now and get dressed. I'd like you to come down to my office after they take fluids from you again."

~ ~ ~

Darby sat across from the physician in an office that looked more like a runaway storage space. The politician felt as though he had to peek between the charts and books stacked on the doctor's desk to see Dr. Smith's face. Lacing his fingers together in a prayer like gesture, the doctor delivered his diagnosis. Darby was in acute renal failure. Such a serious diagnosis required a second opinion, maybe even a third, and the general practitioner located a sheet of paper with kidney specialists on it.

"They're listed in ranked order, which is subjective, I know," the doctor said, passing the list, "but you can't go wrong contacting any of the names on there. It is imperative that you contact someone right away. Your symptoms have kind of snowballed rapidly, and we need to see if we can get ahead of this as soon as possible. Whoever you choose will want to do their own workups and lab work. I know how much you enjoy that, but it's for the best. I'll send over your history as soon as you find someone."

The doctor stood and stuck out his hand. "Good luck."

As Darby retrieved his car from the multilevel parking garage, it was Dr. Smith's "good luck" that scared him the most. He called his wife immediately after paying his toll.

"I'm coming home," he said. "Dr. Smith says I need a specialist. It's probably some sort of fee-splitting arrangement he's got worked out with some guys he went to school with, but it's better to err on the side of caution, right?"

His wife agreed that erring on the side of caution was prudent. An hour later, she was calling the first name on the list to get her husband an appointment. Using the cudgel of his title, "State Senator Darby Clements" got scheduled for a week from that Thursday. He was requested not to eat anything after midnight and to avoid drinking anything but water on the day of the visit.

In what he would later describe as "whistling past the graveyard," Darby threw himself back into his legislation. Feeling that he had received a mandate from his fellow senators, he explored every avenue he could to rid his state of the scourge he saw before him. *Was it enough to just limit their financial opportunities?* he wondered as he sat in his seat in the Senate, staring at the Arkansas flag next to the podium. *Shouldn't there be a registration for all of the people who felt compelled to dress as the opposite sex like there was for other sex offenders?*

What about all of those people who carried the charade to the point of actually getting surgically altered? Shouldn't there be something done to prevent unneeded surgeries?

To that end he sought the advice of one of his fellow senators who also held a medical license. Dr. Sam Browning shared Darby's concern about the loosey-goosey way that gender was being bandied about.

"It's as clear as the nose on your face what a child's sex is at birth." Dr. Sam laughed at his simile. "That's why people scream, 'It's a boy!' or 'It's a girl!' There ain't no denying it at that point."

The septuagenarian enjoyed the company of the junior senator at his table in the Senate lunchroom. Many of his former colleagues had passed away. The rest seemed to just pass by the elder as his viewpoints became more and more didactic. His current crusade involved birth control. It was the doctor's opinion that none was needed, certainly none that was supplemented by the government.

"It's all part of God's plan, you know what I'm saying?" the elder senator said. "All these hormone treatments and other things they're using to keep babies from being born ain't right. Them babies got rights too, and that first right is being born. You know, now that I think on it for a minute, we might have a lot more in common than I originally thought."

"How do you mean?" Darby asked, anxious to get the older man's support.

"I mean what if all of these chemicals and hormones everybody's taken to prevent babies is altering the baby's DNA and making them come out confused?" Senator Sam responded. "I don't know that there's been any long-term studies on what the pill does to the environment that has been more or less pristine since Adam and Eve's time." The senator put down his knife and fork to look Darby square in the eye. "I think what we have here is a shared purpose. You're concerned that there seems to be a preponderance of sexual deviants born into society. Just as important, that these deviants have no shame about it. Like you said, 'They're selling tickets to their perversion.'"

Dr. Sam took a drink of water. "I am concerned that people are fornicating without a thought in their head of the consequences. God made sex a joyful thing for the purpose of procreation. If you're not planning on raising that baby, then abstinence is the path for you. 'Just say no,' Nancy Reagan used to say, and it doesn't just apply to drugs."

The doctor took his glasses off and rubbed the area where they pinched his nose. "But now that we're back to the topic of drugs, what if all of these birth control pills are causing the problems? What if all of these multi-sexers that don't know what they want to be are a byproduct of our experiment with altering God's plan? Yes, my boy, I think we have a common interest."

Darby was confused by the science that Dr. Sam was espousing, but he was convinced that the majority of the Arkansas state legislature didn't care whether the science was empirical or not. The majority of the legislature were white male evangelical Christians with exactly zero tolerance for any opposing views. The Browning-Clements bill passed overwhelmingly. In addition to banning abortions for any reason, it banned the use of any chemical-based birth control. Woven into the bill in language so obscure as to almost be indecipherable was the provision that pediatricians track all patients that suffered "gender assignment disease." A subset of that clause was the creation of a statewide registry to track all individuals who were exhibiting "non–birth gender traits." *It's not everything I hoped for, but it's a good start*, Darby thought when the bill was passed.

Conversely, Darby's health was not going as well as his legislative career. The first blood test at the specialist produced a GFR, or glomerular filtration rate, of 75. The GFR was more indicative of a seventy-year-old, not a man half that age. Darby was placed on a strict diet, urged to drink gallons of water, and exercise hard enough each day to work up a sweat.

"Your kidneys are just one of the ways to get rid of the body's toxins," the specialist advised.

Darby tried to listen. The loss of pork in all of its many forms was hard to take. The loss of salt and alcohol paled in comparison to his mourning the loss of daily barbecue sandwiches and Brunswick stew for lunch. He laughed at the irony of kidney beans being good for the kidneys, but he endured them. He ate more fruit, less junk, and after a few weeks he did feel better. He was in high hopes that his change in lifestyle would result in an immediate improvement. His GFR on his next visit was 70. He was headed in the wrong direction. His doctors ordered an ultrasound and a biopsy.

Darby's kidneys were failing, and the doctors were scrambling for a solution to slow the process. They prescribed diuretics, which Darby hated. Having to run to the bathroom every half hour was hard for a senator. The doctors also prescribed an ACE inhibitor, which helped lower his heart rate but left him tired all the time. Then there were the headaches that left him dizzy.

He occasionally missed roll call even though he was in attendance. The young senator found that he wasn't able to focus on his surroundings like he had before. He was fortunate that the bills he was most interested in were swept in early in the new administration. The legislature had returned to the mundane task of debating which roads to fix, which schools to update, and how the state's districts could be better gerrymandered to insure an even bigger victory for their party at the next election. If there was a good time for Darby to be less energized, this was it.

~ ~ ~

"I'm sorry," the renal specialist, Dr. Sidney Blum said to Darby as he read the chart. "Your creatinine levels keep getting higher. I think we need to look at getting you on the transplant list as soon as possible."

Darby's brain took a spin and nearly crash-dived. "A transplant. You're saying I need a transplant?"

"As soon as possible," the doctor replied. "Unfortunately your blood type is going to be a bit of a problem. B negative is only found in about three percent of the population. Typically, donors come from accidents. I can't mentally calculate the odds of a B-negative person with a signed donor card being in a fatal accident where the kidneys would be viable. That's even before we get to the real problem—how many people with B-negative blood are ahead of you on the list."

"But, I'm a state senator."

Dr. Blum held up his hand to stop Darby's protestations. "Here, read this." He handed Darby a brochure from the National Kidney Foundation.

Darby read the words out loud. "'The United Network for Organ Sharing (UNOS) manages the list of all the people across the US waiting for an organ transplant. UNOS ensures that deceased donor organs are distributed fairly.' What does that mean?"

"It means that each person is evaluated fairly and given their place in line based on the severity of their condition," the doctor answered. "People will move up and down a bit based on certain conditions, but you'll be able to approximate pretty early on when you might get a transplant."

"Is there nothing else we can try? I'm drinking so much water now that I slosh when I walk. I don't eat animal protein. I exercise to a good sweat every day. What else can I do?"

"There's one thing that might help you," the doctor said, rising to meet his next appointment. "There is a directed donor program. If you have a family member or acquaintance with the same blood type who is willing to donate a kidney, then we'll take you right in. There's also a program where a person of a different blood type can donate a kidney to the bank, and that will put you on the top of the list for a kidney of your blood type."

The doctor opened the door. "All is not lost. I've known people to live for years on dialysis, and there's always new drugs and treatments coming down the pike. Hang in there."

Darby stared at the closed door for several minutes before getting dressed. *Who do I know, who do I know?* he asked himself all the way home. He ran through the mental rolodex of all the people he and his wife knew, searching for a potential donor. His parents were dead, and he was the only child of only children. He had always felt lucky growing up that he didn't have to share with anyone else, not even a cousin. Now, he questioned his luck.

Two days later, Darby was notified that his doctor had referred him to the only hospital in the state that did transplants. He immediately made an evaluation appointment. The medical team was kind and knowledgeable. He felt reassured from the visit, but he was left with one nagging concern. The team stressed that his outcome would be greatly enhanced if the transplant could be done before he had to go on dialysis. Darby was frantic to find a donor.

Throwing decorum and tradition to the wind, Darby asked his minister to mention his name in the prayer group at church. Feeling blessed, Darby was heartened to have his name mentioned by the minister during Sunday services. In fact, the minister went on to explain the full process of organ donation to the congregation. Darby's minister mentioned Darby's situation to the other evangelical preachers in the state in a group email that week. Darby had been copied on the email and was proud that the minister had so effusively lauded Darby's work in the Senate and praised him for being such a fine voice for the church. *It would be a shame to lose that voice,* the email read. *If there is just one person who will follow Jesus's teaching to 'love one another as thy self,' then surely they should come forward and save our state senator.*

The transplant coordinator had told Darby to be ready to go at a moment's notice. "If you will be too nervous to drive yourself, make plans. Pack your bag for three days. If you have pets or children, arrange for their care. When we call, we're on the clock, and the success of your transplant is affected by timing. Don't be your own worst enemy."

Darby had taken her words as gospel, and when the call came saying that they had a directed donor, Darby was ready to go. The operation was set for four in the afternoon the next day. The donor wished to remain anonymous, and there was no opportunity for Darby to thank the donor prior to the surgery. While he sat in the prep room waiting for the news that the donor kidney was a healthy match, he reflected over and over on the selflessness of the donor. Darby and his wife had leaned on all her relatives and every acquaintance they knew. No one had come forward. Now, out of the blue came a donor with his blood type.

It's a miracle, plain and simple, Darby thought. *God has a bigger plan for me.*

His thoughts were confirmed when his surgeon came to the prep room to tell him that the surgery was a go. The kidney was a perfect match.

Darby awoke from the surgery uncomfortable but not in too much pain. As his brain cleared, he looked to his wife, who sat dutifully by his side.

"You're awake? Are you OK?" she asked.

Darby nodded to confirm that he was conscious. From the corner of his eye, he saw that he was hooked to a monitor, which was blipping in rhythm to his heart. He could feel that he had an IV running in his arm. His mouth was dry, and he indicated with his free hand to it. His wife responded quickly by placing the straw from a glass of ice water into his lips. Drawing deeply, Darby felt the effects of the anesthesia mask lessen.

As he cleared his throat, his wife interrupted him saying, "I'll go tell them you're awake." She returned with the nurse in tow. The doctor followed a couple of minutes later.

"Mr. Clements, everything went splendid," he said as he reviewed the chart. "If everything goes according to plan, we'll have you out of here in a few days."

The doctor checked the dressings and the little bag on the side of the bed collecting Darby's bodily fluids. "Everything looks fine. You're already 'making water' as we say." He checked Darby's eyes with his little flashlight. "Any complaints?"

"Just really tired. I feel like I could sleep for a week."

"Well, I wouldn't got that far, but I do want you to get plenty of rest for the next two to three weeks," the surgeon said, placing the chart back in its spot. "No lifting, no running marathons, nap as often as you like. Just give everything the chance to settle into place. Keep on the same diet, and we'll add some things back when we see how you're tolerating the new kidney. Any questions?"

"Yes," Darby began. "How is the donor?"

"Just fine. He should be up and walking around tomorrow. All goes well and he'll be out of here the next day, five pounds lighter." The doctor laughed at his own joke and left the recovery area.

Darby slept through the next day and night with only the interruptions of the nurses doing their job. On the third day he joked during his doctor's visit that he was "ready to roll away the rock." His wife laughed, but the doctor didn't catch the reference. He did have a surprise for Darby.

"Your donor is leaving the hospital today and has had a change of heart about being anonymous. He's right outside if you'd like to meet him."

Darby was shocked and thrilled. "Yes, of course, I'd love to meet the man that saved my life."

The door was cleared for the wheelchair to be pushed through. The first thing that Darby noticed about his donor was his eyes. Not his eyes per se, but the shaped eyebrows and long false eyelashes. Darby's mouth flew open, which allowed the donor the opportunity to extend his hand in greeting. The donor's long nails were colored blood red with little rhinestones artistically attached.

"I am so pleased to meet you," the donor said as he gave Darby's hand a little squeeze. "It's not often in life we are given the opportunity to actually save someone else's life, and I did it. I saved your life. John 15:13. 'Greater love has no one than this, that someone lay down his life for his friends.' I mean, we're not friends yet, but I hope we will be. And I guess I didn't die, but I could have, so the thought was there. Anyway, I just wanted to meet you and make sure you were taking good care of my kidney. Our kidney."

Darby was speechless.

LIVE LONG ENOUGH

The septuagenarian repeated the words over and over to himself. *If you live long enough, you'll live forever.* It had been fifty years since Alonzo Symmes had heard the CEO of the largest tech company in the world throw away the comment at a conference in Malaysia. Alonzo was attending the conference as a wunderkind chip developer. Not satisfied with the constraints of Moore's Law, which stated that the number of transistors on a microchip doubles every two years and that the speed and capability of our computers will increase every two years because of this, yet we will pay less for them, Alonzo had decided to make more Moore.

He designed a chip that was based on the von Neumann architecture. The chip utilized the von Neumann architecture's primary advantage, simplifying the microcontroller chip design so that only one memory was accessed. The biggest asset for the microcontrollers was that the contents of RAM could be used for both variable (data) storage as well as program instruction storage, like the human brain. The von Neumann architecture consisted of processing, control, memory, input, and output units. *Just like the human brain*, Alonzo had thought when he attended class at MIT. *Now how do we make it small enough to fit into a human skull?*

Moore's Law helped with the fit issue. Over the fifty years that Alonzo worked to deliver the perfect chip, petabytes of information, one thousand terabytes, could be stored on an area the size of a pinhead. *The problem is not the fit,* Alonzo thought as he reflected back on the days of rooms filled with massive boxes that had less computing power than a modern toy. *The problem is how to get the data there.* He took off his VR glasses, signaling to his helper that he was done for the evening. *And the essence. The data is nothing without the essence.*

The helper wheeled Alonzo into the dining room, where his family waited for his birthday celebration. At seventy-nine, Alonzo could smile with pride about most of his accomplishments. His five children, by three wives, beamed back at him. His fourth wife smiled from the opposite side of the glass table. Alonzo was wheeled to the head of the table, which sat on a glass floor that gave an unobstructed view of the city street a thousand feet below. The dining room had been added to the penthouse apartment at considerable cost. Alonzo had joked when giving the specifications to the architect that he wanted people to have a place to look during those awkward silences that are often found at family gatherings. The architect was happy to oblige, as were the construction crews. The resulting skyscraper was commonly referred to as "the wart" for the growth that jutted out from the face of the building.

"Thank you all for coming," Alonzo addressed the group. "I know some of you are surprised to be here. Yes, I've made it another year."

A nervous twitter escaped the group as they looked back at their benefactor.

Alonzo looked at the group that would be his human legacy. His true legacy was his work, the thousands of jobs he had created and the changes to civilization that were a direct result of his genius. Alonzo's breakthroughs in chip design came at the same time that artificial intelligence was just beginning to learn to crawl. Over the course of Alonzo's life, AI had learned to run at a dizzying speed.

It was this synergism that had produced the first autobots, humanlike machines that could physically replace humans in a variety of environments. From librarians to food service to factory workers, the autobots were not only capable of doing mundane tasks without boredom but could be moved from one task to another without the need to design and make a new specialized robot for the task. Like their human predecessors, the autobots just needed to be introduced to the task, and then they took over for the human. Their "brains" accessed all the relevant information about the task from the internet and refined their internal programs down to the most efficient way to perform the task. Utilization refined the methods, and the Perfect Task Manual would be created and stored for future implementations.

As Alonzo looked at his family, he wished that AI had been further along when his first wife had divorced him. Nanny-bots had played a greater part in the development of the younger members of the group. The nanny-bots utilized by Alonzo and wives two and three were deficient in many qualities needed to make children secure in their surroundings. As a result, the younger three children were far more dependent on their trust funds for survival.

If I was around more, perhaps I would have seen the problems, made course changes. He clinked his glass for attention. *But if I had been around more, we wouldn't be here now. A man has to trade some things in life, make some concessions if he is going to accomplish his dreams, and I am almost there.*

He cleared his throat. "Thank you all very much for coming. I have a little news item to discuss with everyone while you eat your cake."

"We'd like to be served," he said to the two service-bots standing at the buffet table next to a four-layer cake in the shape of an 8080 microchip. The servers placed the cake on the table in front of Alonzo and lit the two candles in the shape of a 7 and 9. The group responded by singing a hearty version of "Happy Birthday" while Alonzo leaned as close as he could to enable his failing lungs the ability to blow out the candles. With a mighty "whoosh" he accomplished his task and fell back into his chair from the effort. The group applauded his effort, and the service-bots placed generous portions of the cake in front of the participants.

Ignoring his cake, Alonzo leaned forward and took a deep breath. "This past year has been one filled with small successes and large failures. The failures have been various organs, and my doctors tell me that very soon I will have to be connected to external machines to do the work that my internal organs should be doing."

He watched the faces around the table for reactions. To his surprise, they all seemed to be genuinely concerned.

"As some of you know I've been working on an AI project while I've been stuck at home dealing with my health issues." Alonzo looked directly at his eldest son. "I'm getting close to beta testing. In fact, I think I'm close enough to be able to share my project with my family." Alonzo rose up in his chair so that his voice would carry farther. "A.II., will you come in here please?"

The group turned to watch a bot come from the direction of Alonzo's lab. The similarity of the bot to its creator was startling. The skin tone was perfect, as were the eyes and the hair. The bot walked fluidly to stand at the head of the table. A.II., or Alonzo 2, smiled and greeted each of the family members by name. Only the two oldest children replied in kind. A.II. seemed pleased at their acknowledgment.

Alonzo studied his family's reaction before speaking. His eldest showed no surprise and seemed to have a self-satisfied smile on his face. The others looked shocked. Alonzo couldn't tell whether it was the bot's fourth-generation skin or that A.II. so closely resembled him at age thirty that had thrown his family into stupefaction.

"Well, what do you all think?" Alonzo asked. "Anybody want to arm-wrestle my double? I will warn you, he has the strength of ten."

There were no takers.

"Aww, come on," Alonzo implored. "Asimov's three laws of robotics will protect you. I think. We put those into your programming, didn't we?" Alonzo turned to A.II.

"Yes, sir, I believe you did," A.II. responded. "A robot may not injure a human being or, through inaction, allow a human being to come to harm. A robot must obey orders given to it by human beings except where such orders would conflict with the First Law. A robot must protect its own existence as long as such protection does not conflict with the First or Second Law."

"And are you a robot?" Alonzo asked.

"Yes, sir," A.II. answered. "But a very special one. I am unique in that I will be the very first replica of a human. You, sir."

A.II. smiled at the group. The group continued to stare back at the wonder with their mouths open. As if he sensed the group's discomfort, A.II. began to speak again. "I am the result of years of study, nearly a billion dollars in costs, and technological advances only dreamed of months ago. My outer shell is a living skin developed by the Xenex labs for burn victims. It is subject to all the frailties of human skin. Cuts, bruises, sunburn, blisters. I don't get warts, though. I guess that's a blessing."

Jonah, the third child, rose from his chair and walked directly to A.II. His nose a half an inch from A.II., he looked deeply into the bot's eyes.

Holding his gaze, A.II. began to speak. "My eyes are but one of my input devices. They are designed to not only look real but to provide me with vision under any circumstance. I can see in the dark, under water, and through smoke. The images are interpreted by my central processor, and I use what my creator calls 'best judgment' to evaluate what action, if any, is needed."

Suddenly Jonah grabbed a piece of A.II.'s cheek and twisted it.

"Owww," A.II. responded. "If I am to interpret your action correctly, I believe you were testing another one of my input devices. Yes, I feel things. Was that your test?"

"Answer him," Alonzo said. "It's important to his sense of self to know that you were testing him and not being a brat."

"Yeah, it was a test," Jonah said as he returned to his chair. "You passed."

"I am pleased. Thank you," A.II. responded.

Alonzo looked around the room. "Anyone else want to act out?"

While the blank stares had been replaced by looks of concern, there were no other volunteers.

"OK, here's the deal," Alonzo began. "A.II. has been going to school for quite a while. His course of study has been my brain. While we're on the topic of tests, feel free to ask him anything about me. Dates, times, places, events, and most importantly, feelings."

Alonzo turned to his second child, his daughter Janey. "Janey, ask him about the day you were born."

Janey looked up apprehensively. "A.II., tell me about the day I was born."

A.II. recited the date and time in a tone similar to a digital clock, but then his voice softened.

"Well, dear," A.II. began. "It was snowing like it would never stop. When your mom said it was time to go to the hospital, I was scared we'd never find a cab. We didn't have a car and a driver back then like we do now. We relied on the city's transit system to get around. Every penny we could spare went into the business in those days, and it was before my first big contract. I was terrified that we wouldn't get to the hospital on time. But we did."

A.II. paused and smiled directly at Janey. "What a surprise you were. Six pounds and fifteen ounces of screaming fury. You weren't happy when you got here, but by the time we left the hospital, you'd turned into the sweet little Bumpus you've been ever since. Men always think about their legacy, of having a son to carry on the family name, but I can tell you, there is no feeling like holding your daughter for the first time."

To everyone's surprise, Janey had started crying. It was during A.II.'s recitation of her birth that Janey realized what her father and older brother had been working on all their lives. She had accepted the fact that her brother had followed their dad into the family business, and that there were secrets that only they would share, but this was something else. This was way beyond developing smart chips for bots. This was about making bots more humanlike. *It's even more than that*, Janey thought. *This is next level. This is creepy.*

The rest of the party were recovering their senses. Winston, the youngest, turned to A.II. and said, "Now do me."

Alonzo cut A.II. short. "Let's wait a bit before we walk down memory lane with all of you. Let me make clear, if I know it, A.II. knows it. Three years ago, I had a receptor-transmitter planted in the thalamus of my brain. Since then, all the signals being sent to my brain from any of my five senses have also been sent to A.II. Those signals are then stored as data. With Junior's help, we've been able to refine that input to my brain into memories in A.II.'s brain. With a lot of teaching, we have helped A.II. to interpret the signals as we think I would. He is trained to be in 'deference mode' while in my presence, but if I were to leave the room, his actions should be the same as I would make."

Alonzo nodded toward his helper. "And that's what we're going to test. I'm going to leave the room, and you will continue to enjoy my party with A.II. as host. All the memories of the party from this point forward will be his memories. Our neural link only goes one way. I'll study the CCTV footage to build an assessment of A.II.'s interpretations of the party compared to my own observations. I'm hopeful that our interpretations will integrate seamlessly."

The helper began wheeling Alonzo in his ancient wheelchair from the room.

"Thanks for coming," he called as he left.

The next hour and a half was spent with the group trying to test A.II.'s capabilities. Legitimate queries were interspersed with test questions hoping to invoke a false memory of A.II. "Do you remember the time . . ." was answered over and over with the correct response. Either A.II. would recite a correct recounting of the event or reply, "That never happened." Finally, the group became bored with the interview and started trickling away from the party one by one. Just A.II., the two oldest children, and the current wife were left.

"What's Dad trying to do?" Janey asked her brother.

"He's trying to live forever," replied Alonzo Jr.. "It sounds like something out of a Mary Shelley novel, but he's very close."

"Close. Close how?" Janey retorted. "His body looks like a balloon with most of the air let out. He's just sitting around here all day tinkering with his toys. If he wants to live longer, he should be exercising, getting out in the world, eating healthier, not staying cooped up here in his ivory castle."

"Maybe thirty years ago that might have been true," Junior answered. "But truth be told, the old man doesn't have much time left. That's why this party was so important. We needed to introduce A.II. to the family. We needed to gauge everyone's reaction."

"Why?" Janey asked. "When he's gone, he's gone and that's it. You and I will inherit the business, and everyone else will have a trust fund to mismanage. No offense." The last comment was directed at stepmother number three.

"None taken," replied the woman. "You kids let yourself out, I'm going to bed. Nothing else important to learn here." She patted A.II. on its head and shuffled out of the room.

Junior waited for his stepmother to leave before beginning again. "We're doing things that are unheard of. We've broken ground in so many areas of consciousness and neural pathways that we don't even have the time to file all of the patents. Don't worry, I'm keeping my documentation, and at some point, I will file them. It's just that right now A.II. is learning on an exponential level. He is actually guiding our path now."

Janey turned and looked directly at A.II., who in turn, smiled back at her. Unnerved, she asked the question anyway. "And what's in this for you? You don't legally exist. You can't own property; you can't sit on the board of directors. You're just a home movie with a great file system. You may be the physical embodiment of Dad in his thirties, but you're not Dad."

A.II. furrowed his brow as he "thought" about his answer. "No, not yet, but soon."

The anthropomorphism exhibited by A.II. stalled Janey's plunge into the pool of everything that was wrong with her father's plan. As she collected her thoughts, Junior interjected the showstopper.

"We think we've located the soul," he began slowly. "Dad likes to call it his 'essence.' Call it potato if you like, but we think we've isolated that thing that makes us all uniquely different."

Janey dropped her head in her hands on the table while emitting a guttural "Argggh!"

Junior couldn't tell if his sister was locked in an existential battle in her own mind or just watching the street traffic a thousand feet below as a diversion to the discussion. He waited patiently while she caught up to the conversation.

Rubbing her hands through her hair, the family trait that probably caused premature baldness, Janey rose back up to a full seated position. She turned her attention to A.II. and looked deeply into the bot's eyes. "You think you've found the soul?"

"Yes," A.II. replied. "There will be more tests, of course, but we're within a margin of error of four percent. Given the time that we believe we have left, we feel confident that we are there."

Janey turned back to her brother. "Let's forget this soul business. I much prefer Dad's word, 'essence.' Outside of this overgrown calculator's word for it, what makes you think that being human is captured in what we will be forever calling 'essence'?"

"Einstein said, 'Energy cannot be created or destroyed. It can only be changed from one form to another,'" Junior replied. "It was how he answered questions about the afterlife from people who wouldn't take no for an answer."

"I thought he said that he didn't believe in the immortality of the individual."

"He did say that, but that's where we think we may have an advantage on his perspective," Junior answered. "There have been studies that show that immediately after death the body loses weight."

"Oh my god!" Janey shrieked. "Are you talking about that stupid twenty-one-gram theory that was disproven years ago? Is this the empirical evidence that you're using to spend billions of dollars and waste Dad's remaining time? I can't believe I'm hearing this!"

A.II. cleared his throat or made a sound that was designed to mimic the clearing of one's throat. "No, Janey, that's not what we're talking about. Eastern religions have taught for thousands of years that humans, or their essence, come back again and again. They are reincarnated or given a new body so that they can finish the work that was left undone in their previous life. At least, that is the premise."

Janey looked at the machine incarnation of her father and raised an eyebrow. "Really?"

"I can see that you're skeptical," A.II. continued, "but consider the innumerable accounts of people recalling past lives. Where did that knowledge come from? Why are humans born with innate fears of snakes, spiders, and politicians?"

Janey looked at the smile on A.II.'s face and knew that he knew he had made a joke. It was not the recitation of a knock-knock joke; it was a humorous spin, an ad lib. Janey turned to her brother to avoid the paternal smile of the bot. Junior was looking up at the CCTV that was covering the room. *Was Junior making sure that Dad caught A.II. making a joke?* Janey wondered.

"OK, say you have a measurement for the weight of one's essence," Janey said. "Did Henry VIII's essence weigh more than Gandhi's? Does an adult's essence weigh more than a child's? Does yours weigh more than mine?"

Junior looked perplexed for a moment and then answered, "Oh no, not that kind of weight. We're talking about atomic weight and the number of particles that comprise a pea-size area that is deep within the thalamus. We discovered it when we were installing Dad's receptor-transmitter. We've found nothing about it in any medical books. It's right there where all inputs and outputs take place but doesn't seem to have any function. It doesn't control anything; it doesn't send any messages anywhere. It doesn't seem to be large enough to store much memory, but our experiments have us convinced that this little pea-brain is where the essence resides."

Janey looked back and forth between her brother and her pseudo father and declared, "You all are certifiably cuckoo, nuts, whatever you've got programmed in his brain. You have gone around the bend, and you're not taking me on the ride with you." She rose to leave.

"Wait a minute," Junior said. "We need to talk a little bit more. You're right—Dad's not doing well. We've been working frantically so that we can control the timing of things. We want to make the transfer while Dad's still alive."

Janey sat back down. "Transfer, what transfer?"

Junior took a big breath. "We believe, and our experiments have led us to conclude, that at the time of death, the essence, those atomic particles that make us, us, leave the body and return to the universe. That like Einstein said, energy never dies, it just changes form. Once back in the universe, the essence looks for another living host to attach to and continue its work."

Janey looked back and forth between her brother and A.II. "You've just described, poorly, *Invasion of the Body Snatchers*. Next, I guess you're going to tell me that you're going to shortcut the process by cutting out part of Dad's brain and planting it in this life-size replica of him?"

Junior reached his arm around his sister's shoulders. "Yes, that's exactly what we're going to do. We're going to use the same team that did the receptor-transmitter implant. We've prepared a living tissue host in A.II. and we feel like we can maintain the environment in perpetuity. Dad will live forever, and eventually so will you and I, and anyone else that can afford the process."

Janey took her brother's arm from her shoulders and once more headed for the door. "You're nuts. I don't know what's legal and what's not, but I certainly have a feeling for what's ethical and moral. Count me out, now and later."

At a great cost, Alonzo and Alonzo Jr. paid for a live run-through. Two healthy candidates were chosen from the local homeless shelter and offered ten million dollars each for the operation that would change not only their outward appearance but the essence of who they were. The legal contract was over forty pages long. It was explained that whatever physical maladies existed in the host's body prior to the operation would be inherited by the new definitive host. If successful, the patient would recognize all his family and be able to recall all the events of his previous life, but there were no guarantees.

Alonzo and his son were hopeful that there would be no bleed over of memories from one host to the next. During one particularly stressful strategy session A.II. postulated the idea that both patients might result in a synergism of both hosts. There could be two distinctly different hosts with exactly the same personalities and memories. "Would the operation be a success or failure if that happened?" A.II. had posed. Alonzo and his son agreed that for the purposes of the experiment it would be considered a failure, while agreeing that for their personal needs it would be deemed a success.

The living tissue transferred into A.II.'s cranium had taken root successfully and was as much a part of him as his skin. This living tissue would be the organic home for what the team were now referring to as the "Essentia." The name was selected by A.II. after Junior complained that the team couldn't keep calling the organ the "pea." Whether the name ever made it into medical journals would be determined by the success or failure of the donor swap.

The trial surgery was scheduled for the first of June. If all went well, Alonzo's transplant would occur on June 19, his birthday. All eyes were focused on Alonzo's failing health. Many times, Junior thought he would have to call the transplant team and say that the test case would have to be his dad. Each time, Alonzo would rally and will himself to be an integral part of the team. It was his life's work, and he didn't want to punk out right at the end. Finally, June 1 came, and the surgery began.

To everyone's amazement, the surgery was easier than the rehearsals. The Essentia was transferred between the patients, who were lying side by side in the operating room. Five hours after putting the patients under anesthesia, they were wheeled into the recovery area. An hour later the patients were wheeled to separate rooms for their postoperative interview. Each patient was given a series of questions pertaining to their former identities and from their host's identities.

In the interviews given immediately after surgery, both identities seemed to be at the core of the subject's being. As time progressed, the new identities asserted their dominance. Periods of sleep seemed to accelerate the process, and by the following morning the transference was complete. "Tom was Tim, and Tim was Tom" was how the team joked about their success when recounting it to others.

What puzzled the team was the full overlap of personalities at first and the part that sleep played in the eventual resolutions of the identities. A.II. did a deep dive on the internet for all things metaphysical.

"I think I have it," A.II. said to Alonzo and Junior in the lab at the penthouse. "It's a theory, but there are a lot of religions and superstitions that are explained by my interpretation. What if there is a 'Universal Consciousness,' a repository for all things associated with sentient life? What if the Essentia is a receptor-transmitter to the Universal Consciousness, and the Universal Consciousness is like the cloud for the internet? Then we would see that the human brain is local storage that updates, and is updated by, the cloud. The Essentia is like a node on a network. It has an address that the cloud keeps track of and makes sure that the data matches the location."

"So, when our subjects woke up," Alonzo began, "they still had local memory stored in their brains from their former selves, but gradually the cloud updated their memories with the data that was assigned to that address."

"Yes," A.II. responded. "From a metaphysical point of view, it would explain so much. Remembering past lives, astral projection, prior learning, so many things. I am still unresolved on the significance of physical birth. There must have been an original birth for the Essentia to be available to the universal consciousness. What I've not resolved is what the numbers mean. Are there billions of souls waiting in the cloud to be reborn?"

A.II. looked from Alonzo to Junior for an answer. "In 2050 the Earth's population was 10 billion. While concerning on an environmental level, that's not the most disturbing number for our purposes. The important number, in my opinion, is that the estimate for births since man emerged is 121 billion. Are there 110 billion souls floating in the ether waiting for a host? Is what we're doing going to stop rebirth and therefore spiritual growth? Are we going to upset a plan that may extend to other universes, other species? Are we not playing God?"

Father and son looked at each other and then at A.II. After a few stressful seconds, Alonzo responded, "I don't know, I just don't know."

~ ~ ~

On June 19, Alonzo's eightieth birthday, the operation took place transferring his soul, his essence, the Essentia, into A.II. Alonzo did not recover from the anesthesia. A.II. was "awake" the whole time. Father and son had debated pre-surgery whether to put A.II. into sleep mode for the procedure. It was decided that his insight might be helpful to all. A.II. was conscious when his brain was connected to "the cloud."

The universal consciousness set about updating A.II. with the data from over a thousand lives lived in multiple universes. His storage was quickly overrun. The error message that would have been displayed in the early days of computing was an Error 61(Disk full). A.II. was left in the memories, the life, of a man named John Aed who lived in County Cork, Ireland, in 1512.

The modern world came as quite a shock to the shepherd.

UNDER THE BRIDGE

The rain fell slowly and thickly. Each drop was ice cold, as if it had been sleet a second before. The torrential rain blanketing the area had been frozen water until it passed through the last few yards of the stratosphere falling to earth. The temperature at ground level was just above freezing. That would change as night encroached.

The group of people standing under the interstate bridge were huddled around a fire burning in a fifty-five-gallon oil drum. There was not enough room around the fire for everyone at once, so they took turns warming their hands. The only child in the group was held securely by her mother. The fire was not the only danger.

The social worker walked slowly toward the group. She knew that she had been spotted as soon as she had parked her car. The lookout would have alerted the group that she was not immigration or a member of law enforcement.

"Hola, cómo están?" she called to the group as she approached.

"Hola," responded some of the group.

The social worker walked directly to the woman with the child. "Hola, niña. Cómo estás?" The child retreated deeper into her mother's arms. She appeared to be about eight years old, but it was hard to approximate based on size. The social worker gave a little tickle to the child's back in an attempt to bond with her and her mother. The child was not wearing a coat, and her exposed skin was taking on a bluish tinge. Reflexively, the social worker took off her coat and wrapped it around the mother and child.

"Me llamo Paula Walker," the social worker said, introducing herself. "Dónde está tu esposo?"

"Mi esposo está en Guatemala," replied the young woman as she changed shoulders with her child.

"Si viene conmigo, cuidaré de ustedes," Paula said to the woman, assuring her that she would take care of her and her child if she would come with her.

The woman sized up the situation and grabbed her duffel bag. "Me llamo Maria y ésta es Elena."

Maria and Elena. She'd get the rest of the details when they got to the shelter. For now, she was happy that the woman had placed her faith in her. She turned the heat up full blast in the car as they rode toward downtown. The child's skin was beginning to regain a pinkish hue. The music from Radio Salsa played on the radio. Seeing the child's reaction to the tunes, Paula turned it up a little louder and sang along.

The trip to the shelter passed quickly. Once inside, Paula helped her charges fill out the necessary paperwork. When the *papeles necesarios* were completed, Paula showed Maria and Elena to the day-care area. Paula was anxious to see if Elena would relate to any of the toys scattered about the floor. She also wanted to observe Elena's reaction to other children. Telling Maria that she would watch Elena, Paula handed Maria a cell phone and encouraged her to call her husband. Paula watched Elena play while surreptitiously listening to Maria tell her husband the horrors of the trip.

The semitrailer that Maria and Elena had been loaded into in Guatemala City had been packed with emigrants of every size and description. Maria calculated that there were sixty other people in the trailer trying to flee their homes for a better life. She fairly screamed to her husband that the coyote was making about three hundred thousand dollars for the trip. The bathroom breaks were nonexistent, and the food and water breaks were once a day. The twenty-five-hundred-mile journey had taken a week, twice as long as promised. The description of horrors went on for about ten minutes. Finally, Maria calmed down enough to tell her husband that she and Elena were safe, and they had made a friend. Paula was very happy to hear the last part. Maria finished the conversation by reading all the information from Paula's business card to her husband. "Te amo mucho," Maria said and handed the phone back to Paula.

They collected Elena and walked down the hall to the dormitories. The room was outfitted with two sets of bunk beds, two wardrobes, two chests of drawers and two desk sets. Paula assured Maria that she and Elena would be the only occupants for a while. The furniture was modest, but everything was disinfected clean. Most importantly, the room was warm, and there was a lock on the door.

They dropped off the duffel bag containing all their worldly possessions and followed Paula to the dining hall. She pointed out the common bathroom and showers as they approached the great room. They pushed through the giant metal doors into a very large room that appeared to have been a gymnasium at one time. Paula explained that the shelter had once been an elementary school until the demographics for the area had changed. The former lunchroom of the school was not large enough to accommodate the groups of people that came off the street daily for food and lodging. The room had been divided into about 60 percent cots and 40 percent dining tables.

The "residences," where Maria and Elena would be living, were accessed by a robust key card system. Paula handed Maria her personalized key card and showed her how it worked. "Solo para ti. No compartas," Paula cautioned Maria. *For you only. Don't share.*

As Maria surveyed the room filled with homeless of every description, every stage of mental health, Paula could see that Maria was taking her cautions to heart. "Sí, solo para mí. No voy a compartir." *Yes, just for me. I will not share.* Basic security settled, Paula pushed the mother and daughter toward the buffet line.

Paula was always amazed at how the children would fill their plates to the brim and do their gut-busting best to clean their plates. Either from decorum or a sense of concern that the next person in line might not have enough, the parents generally took smaller portions no matter how long they had been without. Maria had not taken enough food to keep a bird alive, and Paula told her so. Paula encouraged her to go back into the line until Paula felt that Maria would sleep through the night with a full feeling.

Satisfied that the pilgrims were full, Paula took them back into the residences to introduce them to the commissary. The commissary was filled to the brim with clothing and personal items that could be purchased for the low, low price of *gratis*.

"Gratis?" asked Maria as they chose a nice winter parka for Elena.

"Gratis," Paula replied. They moved to the apothecary area to pick up toiletries and other personal items.

A quick trip to the library, which was vastly improved from its elementary school days, opened the door for Elena to Dr. Seuss and learning English in a fun way. The room was outfitted with a dozen or so laptops that provided the internet on a first-come, first-served basis. A TV sat in each corner of the room, with headsets to maintain the sanctity of the environment. It was a calm sanctuary where they could learn about their new country.

Having been exposed to "the important stuff," Paula returned the pair to their room.

"You are free to walk around the secure area," Paula told Maria. "Most people hang out in the library or their rooms except for mealtime. Elena can go to the day care to play if you'll stay with her to make sure she does OK. Tomorrow we'll see what we can do about finding you a job so that you and Elena can get a place of your own."

Many *muchas gracias* were said between tears and hugs. With a last "OK?" Paula returned to the main office.

~ ~ ~

"Are you heading back out?" The voice came from the other side of her cubicle wall.

"Yeah, we're supposed to get freezing rain tonight. I thought I'd make a swing by all of the usual spots before calling it a day."

Paula's "cell mate," Todd Bowers, peeked around the corner of the cubicle. "Well, I wanted to give you this before you left." He handed Paula a poorly wrapped package. "Merry Christmas. I know we're just supposed to do the secret Santa thing, but we sit next to each other, and I felt like it was something you wouldn't buy for yourself."

"You're right," Paula replied with a laugh, holding the magnifying glass up for approval. "Never in a million years would I buy one of these for myself." She trained the glass on one of the government publications outlining how they were to perform their jobs. "Oh my god," she exclaimed. "I can actually read this thing. I'm not sure if that's a good thing or not. I might find out I've been doing my job all wrong for all of these years."

"Trust me," Todd said as he reached in for a hug, "you're doing the job exactly the right way. You make all of us proud to be here."

Paula wiped the tear from her eye with her index finger and smiled back at Todd. "I had the best teacher one could ever hope for. Thanks so much and Merry Christmas."

She left the shelter and drove a circuitous route around the city, looking in the homeless encampments for children in distress. Her trip was fruitless, which was Paula's idea of a good run. The snow was beginning to fall. It would be the rarest of things to have a white

Christmas. *There's always hope*, she thought to herself. *The children do love a white Christmas.*

She arrived back home, one block from the shelter, well after dark. Her apartment was clean and tidy. The furnishings were spartan, much like the shelters. The one extravagance was an enormous aquarium occupying one wall. She walked over and sprinkled a small amount of food across the surface. The guppies responded quickly with a dazzling display of colors as they attacked the food. She sat on the ottoman, watching them feed until she was sure they were done. All of her pets taken care of, she set about satisfying her own hunger. The microwave finished its work quickly, and Paula devoured her dinner almost as quickly.

Lying awake in her bed that night with the anxiety of a child on Christmas Eve, Paula reflected on what she considered to be her first peaceful Christmas. Her mother had dropped her off at the newly opened Wee Care day care center, which was funded by an outlier church group. Most of the children were Hispanic. Paula was one of the few Anglo children thrown into the mix. The dominant demographic were children of migrants being exploited by the local agriculture and poultry industries.

Paula's sense of not belonging would have been even more profound if not for the attention she received from the director of the Wee Care centers, Mulva Lyte. "Miss Mulva" made everyone feel special, as if they belonged. When Paula's mother did not return to pick her up that day, Miss Mulva seized the moment and took Paula home with her. They were going to "have a sleepover." It was two weeks before Paula's mother's body was identified. Paula was ten.

Miss Mulva applied to be Paula's foster parent and was accepted. When Paula was twelve, the Lytes offered to adopt her as their own. Paula accepted the offer happily with one provision: she wanted to keep her mother's name. Paula wanted to keep the link to the person that society would judge as having done the "wrong thing." Paula knew that what her birth mother had done was ultimately the right thing. It took a while, but eventually the Lytes became "Mom" and "Pop."

The years passed quickly, and Paula learned to speak Spanish fluently from her playmates. She learned compassion and an unceasing work ethic from the Lytes. The university provided a degree in social work but, more importantly, taught Paula the importance of grants. Paula left college with the ability to wring money from the most penny-pinching curmudgeon. "You can catch more flies with honey than with vinegar," Mom had always told her.

Paula would use a version of honey mixed with the opportunity to "create a positive social presence" when appealing to potential donors. Most donors were more concerned with the positive press than having a positive effect. Paula was OK with that. "We've all got our reasons," she always replied to critics of their donors.

She woke at about four that Christmas morning and drove the short distance to the shelter. There she met Todd and a couple of other die-hard do-gooders who were in the teacher's lounge-conference room. The group added the final touches to the Christmas tree and festooned it with decorations and envelopes. The envelopes were addressed to the current occupants of the residence and contained gift cards chosen specifically for their needs. Presents chosen especially for each of the residents were placed under the tree.

Paula had selected a particular doll for Elena from the shelter's warehouse of donated goods. The "La Baby" had Hispanic features and coloring. She argued with herself as to whether a child who had just completed a twenty-five-hundred-mile trek from an area that was not child friendly would appreciate a baby doll. Had Elena's life experience already forced her to outgrow the need for dolls? Paula was delighted to find out that she had been wrong to doubt her decision.

Elena had a look on her face that could come only from a child receiving just what she wanted from Santa Claus. Paula's face had almost the same look as she watched Elena hug the doll tightly to her body. She used her phone to take a picture of the ecstatic child. She sent the picture to Mom with the message, *The gift that keeps on giving.* Mom texted right back three smiley-face emojis. *Drive carefully when you come, the roads are slippery.*

~ ~ ~

Christmas was the happy time, when all the hard work for the year culminated into one day of festivity, joy, and glad tidings. Too soon the holiday was over, and a new year of goals and expectations was upon them. Grants to be written, tours of the facility given to prospective donors, tons and tons of paperwork that all had to be done in order to do what Paula wanted to do the most: help people. Through it all she continued to make her daily tours through the homeless cities that had sprung up all about the area. Her focus was narrow—children and their mothers—but she felt that long term that was where her resources would have the most impact. She was relieved when the ravages of winter were passed.

~ ~ ~

"How are Maria and Elena adapting to their new roommates?" Todd asked while leaning way back in his chair to clear the cubicle wall between them.

"They're doing OK. They've had a couple of months to learn the ropes, so maybe they can be guides for their new roomies," Paula answered. "Maria is doing well in her new job, so I'm hoping that, with a couple of months' savings, we'll be able to get her into some affordable housing."

"One step at a time, right?" Todd said. "Speaking of which, how are your eye treatments coming? I feel like I've seen you squinting less than usual."

"Well, thanks for noticing, I guess," Paula replied. "I'm probably squinting less because of your gift." She held up the magnifying glass. "I think the damage from malnutrition was done before I got adopted, and I'm just going to have to contend with looking like a mole for the rest of my life."

"Oh, no," Todd responded, flustered. "I didn't mean to imply that there was anything at all wrong with your looks, far from it. I think you look great."

"As long as I don't try to read anything, right?" Paula parried.

"No, actually I was going to ask if perhaps you'd like to read a menu with me some time," Todd countered sheepishly. "We could go Dutch if you have any reservations about us working together."

"Let me think about it," Paula said as she gathered her purse. "I appreciate the offer though. I'm going to make a run and then cruise by Maria's work and see if I can gain some insight into her long-time employment prospects before we commit her to a lease."

"Oh, OK. Be safe," Todd answered, and pushed back into the depths of his cubicle.

The air was crisp and clean as Paula strode across the parking lot to her car. She was getting an early start on her rounds; Todd's invitation to dinner had unnerved her. She went on the occasional date, and there was nothing wrong with Todd. In fact, he was quite a nice guy. It was just that his insight into her personal condition made her feel uneasy. Calling attention to it by giving her a magnifying glass for Christmas could have been taken as a cruel act. Paula didn't feel that it was, but she was disquieted by his interest. Their work was important, indeed, the most important thing in the lives of the people they helped. There was little time now to focus on one's personal desires. *That can come later*, she thought. *Maybe*.

The thought of a romantic entanglement reminded her of the time Pop had inquired about her lack of a date at Thanksgiving dinner. "A woman trying to get through life without a man is like a fish trying to ride a bicycle," he had said. The subsequent fury from the women in the family had caused him to take his plate and retire to the TackyToo rec room for the balance of the day. Since his favorite team was playing on TV, the group knew the colorful version of "a woman is nothing without a man" was more a ploy to get to watch his game in peace rather than a slight. No one knew the power of women better than Bud Lyte.

~   ~   ~

The mattress factory where Maria was employed was one of the go-to places Maria could count on to find employment. They paid immigrants fairly and didn't abuse the employee's situation. The factory was on the same bus line as the high school that taught English for adults, which Maria attended. Her English was coming along nicely, and Paula hoped that she would be able to find Maria a job in her chosen profession. Maria had been a bookkeeper in Guatemala. Everyone agreed that stuffing mattresses all day long was a waste of her education.

"I know the numbers," Maria had told Paula. "I have trouble with the names."

Of course, knowing the names was critical when a business owner asked the bookkeeper to print out the latest P&L or balance sheet. To that end, Paula found Maria an Intro to Accounting class to attend once a week at the local technical school. While the material was old hat for Maria, it gave her the opportunity to learn the names and familiarize herself with American methods. It also gave Paula the opportunity to spend more time with Elena.

There was something about the little refugee that was uniquely special. Elena tugged at Paula's heartstrings more than any of the other children. It wasn't that Elena was more needy, quite the contrary, she was fiercely independent. Her English was making leaps and bounds. Elena insisted that Paula speak to her in English as much as possible. To Paula's surprise, they rarely reverted to Spanish. Words that were new to Elena's vocabulary were given their definitions in English with the rare Spanish translation. She was a very quick study and was soon reading above her grade level in school. Paula beamed with pride when she told Mom and Pop about Elena's accomplishments.

The news about Elena's dad came in a circuitous fashion. Maria and Elena had been buzzing for a week that *Papá* would soon be there. Cinco de Mayo might be a holiday that Maria and Elena would have a cause to celebrate this year. Unfortunately, the group he was traveling with had been discovered by the border agents just eleven miles inside the US border. The authorities used whatever they could find on the bodies to identify the fifty souls abandoned in the semitrailer on the side of the road. Elena's papá had been carrying an envelope and letter from Maria that had the address for the shelter on it. A week had passed from the time he was found until the news reached his family.

The news brought about some of the hardest negotiations Paula had ever been involved in. The arguments were over the deposition of Maria's husband's body. Paula finally convinced Maria that a closed-casket funeral would be necessary. After that decision was made, it became less of a leap to convince Maria that cremation would be the smartest move. Paula made all the arrangements with a funeral parlor in Texas to handle the body and arranged for a memorial ceremony at a local church. The service was surprisingly well attended. Maria and Elena had made a lot of friends inside and outside the shelter community.

Leaving the ceremony with the urn carrying her husband's ashes, the widow seemed consoled that her husband had received a proper ceremony. Elena clung tightly to her mother's skirts after the memorial and was visibly affected by the loss for several weeks. Fortunately, her melancholy didn't last.

~ ~ ~

The one-year anniversary of "being found under a bridge" marked a time of joy and sorrow. Because of Maria's hard work at learning English and American accounting principles, Paula was able to secure her an entry-level job with an accounting firm. The good employment news was tempered by the sad fact that the increase in salary would price Maria and Elena out of the shelter. Fortunately, Paula was able to find an affordable two-bedroom apartment for them in her complex. They would be in a separate building, but close enough that Paula could take Elena to day care at the shelter on those days when school was out.

Paula was also close enough to babysit Elena while Maria continued her education. Maria recognized that her dreams for Elena could be realized by earning a CPA license. Paula was happy to help in any way she could. Elena had seemed to put her sadness behind her and attacked each new day with her old fierceness. She begged Paula to allow her to go on the runs with her to look for displaced children. Paula explained that not all the children that they would encounter were immigrant children. There were a lot of American children that were homeless.

"Is my English not good enough?" Elena inquired.

"It's not that at all," Paula explained. "It's just that their experience is vastly different from yours."

"We both need shelter, we both are hungry, yes?"

"Yes, you're quite right, as usual," Paula smiled. "I'm just warning you that sometimes people don't react the same way to things as you would. I'm just saying be sensitive to that."

Elena considered the advice and begged once again, "When can I go with you? When can I help?"

"Today, right now. Let's go." The pair walked out to the nine-passenger van parked in the shelter's lot.

"You're riding shotgun," Paula said, pointing at the front seat. "I think you're tall enough now, and we need to save the car seat for the bambinos."

With a sense of pride and dignity, Elena buckled herself into what she would forever describe as the "co-captain's chair."

~ ~ ~

It was unseasonably hot that July. "Corn's popping in the fields," Pop had remarked in their weekly call. Paula laughed and assured him that she knew that wasn't true. She did acknowledge that people's moods were as easily affected by bitter heat as they were by bitter cold. "The mission doesn't change because of the season," she reminded him.

The temperature would eventually rise to ninety-nine degrees that July day. Warren Burton went to work as usual. The glass obelisk where he day-traded had tinted its southern exposure to reduce the amount of glare coming through the floor-to-ceiling glass walls. It wasn't the brightness of the sun or the heat that was burning a hole in Warren's brain. It was the recent news delivered by his accountant that his day-trading exploits had left him bankrupt.

Informed at the receptionist desk that his accountant was out for the day, Warren decided that he would not leave the office unsatisfied. Opening his briefcase, he procured the two semiautomatic pistols contained within. Sliding back the bolts on both weapons, he randomly opened fire, killing nine people, one of them a widowed mother who had escaped the violence in Guatemala to give her child the chance at a better life. When the guns were emptied, Warren laid them down and walked out to the street with his hands over his head. He waited for four and a half minutes on a bench at the front of the building before the first police cruiser arrived. He was taken into custody without further incident.

Fifteen minutes away, Elena was helping Paula put away the Fourth of July decorations in the shelter's storeroom. Paula had liberated Elena from her role as "senior helper" in the day care to assist her in reading the fine print on the box labels. Paula's new glasses were strong enough; she just didn't like wearing them everywhere. Also, it was an excuse to spend some time with Elena.

"If we put everything back where it goes, it will be there for us next year," Paula told Elena.

They returned to the shelter's office area to be confronted by the news blaring on the TV. *Nine dead, thirteen wounded,* the chyron read at the bottom of the screen in white letters on a red background. Before Paula could shuttle Elena back to the day care, or any place to shelter her from the horrific scene, a close-up of a sheet-covered body being wheeled out on a gurney appeared on the screen. The TV camera closed in tight on the uncovered left hand of the victim. The close-up shot of the wedding ring lovingly carved from jadeite by her papá revealed the awful truth to Elena.

"Mamá!" she cried.

"Oh god!" cried Paula as she gathered the child in her arms.

"Oh god!" Paula cried again as she held the child close.

COINCIDENCE

It was in that twilight period between administrations, when the outgoing staff was being replaced by the newcomers, that the call came in to the White House Medical Unit. The newly inaugurated president was being rushed to the Eisenhower Executive Office Building for an evaluation. The EEOB, which housed the WHMU, was scant minutes away from the Capitol building where the inauguration was being held. Secret Service decided that the location would provide the very best secure medical services for the newly sworn-in leader.

The government building, originally constructed in 1871, was part of the overall White House compound. In addition to the WHMU, the building housed the offices of the president and vice president, and the National Security Council. Should the evaluation be deemed to be dire, the new president could be airlifted by helicopter to Walter Reed Hospital for further care. The continuity of the government would carry on in the EEOB in his absence. New staff would replace outgoing staff and the nonpolitical government employees. The "bureaucracy" would continue on as if a change had not occurred.

As chief of medical staff James Washington waited on the loading dock of the EEOB, he mused about his role in perhaps the most important moment in history. He grinned inwardly at his hyperbole. *The most important moment in history should be reserved for when something actually happens*, he chided himself. *Still, I could be part of something that has consequences for the whole world.*

Glancing at his watch, he wondered if what was being reported as "the largest crowds of all time" was impeding the progress of the motorcade. He was tempted to go outside to see whether he could catch sight of the automobile affectionately known as "the Beast." Waiting for the patient to arrive was always the worst. He jogged in place for a few steps to ease the tension.

In short order, the Army surgeon would receive a man whose physical condition was known to be poor in spite of the assurances of the politician and his personal physician.

"His physical strength and stamina are extraordinary," the general practitioner had touted in a letter made public. "If elected, Mr. Taint, I can state unequivocally, will be the healthiest individual ever elected to the presidency. Mr. Taint has excellent genes, and if he had taken better care of his diet over the last couple of years, I'm sure he could live to be two hundred."

Dr. Washington knew from the medical records he had received that morning that nothing further from the truth could have been stated. Diabetes, high blood pressure, traces of gout, and a "personal colon issue" indicated that the newly elected president was a man in ill health. The doctor knew from countless articles and TV clips that the new president lived almost entirely off of fast food. The most logical excuse given for living on a diet that every sentient being knew was bad for the body was that the newly elected president feared being poisoned. The politician reasoned that fast food was safe because his assassins would not know in advance which order to poison. The logic was unassailable; the results were horrifying.

Speculating that the dire issue was either a stroke or a heart attack, Dr. Washington was ready to bring forth all the skills he had learned in his three decades in the Army. *The sorry son of a gun is not going to die on my watch*, he thought as the Beast pulled into the loading dock. Two cars filled with Secret Service pulled up on either side of the president's car. The loading dock's bay doors were pulled down to keep prying eyes and nonessential personnel out.

Dr. Washington ran with the gurney team down to the president's car as Secret Service agents helped the behemoth of a man uncoil from the back seat. *He's three hundred and fifty pounds if he's an ounce*, the doctor thought to himself while he attempted to get the man on the gurney. He learned that the man described as six feet, two inches tall wore lifts in his shoes to give the appearance of being much taller. One of the shoes had fallen off in the transfer and lay on its side next to the gurney's wheel. The heel of the loafer was pronounced like the heel on a cowboy boot. *That can't be good for his back.*

"Hello, I'm James Washington, but you can call me J.T. if you like," the doctor said as he took the pulse of the strangely orange-tinted leader of the free world. "We'll get you up to the ER and run some tests and see what's going on. Can you tell me what you're feeling?"

"I'm feeling like I should have called ahead for a reserved spot," the president said before he was cut short by a spasm of pain. The president's body doubled up on the undersized gurney in response to the spasm, causing his highly coiffed hair to fall to one side and reveal a huge bald area that encompassed almost the whole of his head.

My god, he spray tans his bald spot.

"Don't you worry," the doctor said aloud. "You're in the very best of hands here."

The president looked the doctor square in the eye and said, "I doubt that," before crying out in pain again.

The look told the Army colonel all he needed to know about the man whose life he held in his hands. He was a racist.

The man on the gurney being rushed to the operating room embodied everything that James Thomas Washington had had to fight against his whole life. From the hills of West Virginia to the medevac unit in Afghanistan, J.T. had fought prejudice every step of the way to succeed. Now, here he was, caring for "the most powerful man in the world." A man who hated him because of the coincidence of his birth.

~ ~ ~

There were no easy paths for a Black child in Morgantown, West Virginia. J.T. had worked every day for as far back as he could remember to help his family's situation. First as a paperboy and then later doing hourly jobs where his skin color was not found to be objectionable. In high school, he worked as a fry cook at the local fast-food place. He was actually happy not to be working the counter.

It allowed him the opportunity to listen to self-help tapes on his Walkman and concentrate on the video screen displaying the orders.

In this dirt-poor slice of Appalachia, even the white kids were occasionally abused by the customers. Customers who felt their role in life was to elevate their own situation by denigrating others.

One late night, J.T. watched a white girl be pilloried by an outsize, out-of-work coal miner. J.T. took the only action he could to defend the girl who had treated him fairly. As loudly as he could he cleared his sinuses, indicating to one and all that he was about to deposit a large load of phlegm somewhere. That deposit might be into a handkerchief, or it might be into the bun of the triple quarter pounder with cheese that the hillbilly was so anxiously harassing the counter girl about. He turned a curious eye to the customer, who got the message and ended his diatribe. The counter girl, Ellie, also got the message, and a unique bond was formed.

The bond continued through to high school graduation. Diplomas in hand, the pair announced to their parents that they were going to get married and enlist in the Army. The couple explained to their anxious parents that it was their understanding that the Army would try to keep married couples stationed together. Furthermore, it was their plan to attend college with the assistance of the military. Somewhat to their surprise, both sets of parents welcomed their plan and accepted the new member to each of their respective families.

Upon graduation from college, J.T. applied for Officer Candidate School and medical school. He was accepted to both. The military was beginning to see the importance of diversity in the officer corps as well as the ranks. While there were various programs in place to assist candidates of color in achieving their goals, J.T. could proudly claim to have never used his color to his advantage. "Just leave the door open, and I'll earn my seat at the table" was how he described his mindset. He graduated in the top 10 percent of his OCS class and the top third of his medical school. He and Ellie were on the way to achieving their goals of a secure retirement and the opportunity to educate their children in locales around the world.

J.T.'s specialty was general surgery, which placed him in high demand at the Landstuhl Regional Medical Center military hospital in Landstuhl, Germany. While soldiers were surviving the initial trauma on the battlefields of Iraq and Afghanistan at higher rates than ever before, significant repairs still needed to be done to the broken men and women who were airlifted to the LRMC.

J.T. and Ellie were grateful for the opportunities their European station provided. They were especially proud that they were able to educate their children at some of the finest schools in Europe. They were also thankful for how well accepted their biracial children were in the German community. Initial fears of the "white supremacist state" were largely dispelled, and the Washingtons benefitted from the growth of egalitarian views espoused in most of Europe. While the United States was still grappling with Jim Crow, Europe seemed to be forging ahead.

When their last child was accepted to the Sorbonne, the Washingtons were faced with the decision of whether to retire as expats or to return home. The decision was made for them when the United States elected its first Black president. The incoming president's team called, offering J.T. the job of Physician to the

President, which carried with it the title of director of the White House Medical Unit. He happily accepted. Persons of color seeing other persons of color in prominent positions was one of J.T.'s missions. Throughout his career he had taken every speaking engagement offered to him, including the small audiences of his children's classrooms. To J.T., it was vital to let the children know they could rise above their circumstances and other's perceptions.

~ ~ ~

As he looked down at the whale of a man clothed in the colors of the flag J.T. had so proudly served, J.T. pushed the gurney rapidly toward the ER. The blue suit, white shirt, and clownishly long red tie did not fool J.T. The man writhing in pain on the gurney was as much a racist as the originators of the Ku Klux Klan; he was just dressed more appropriately. J.T. was sure there was a robe and hood in XXXXL hanging somewhere.

At the moment the gurney swung into the elevator, the president began to purge violently, adding a kaleidoscope of colors to his patriotic garb. The trauma team was able to avoid much of the spillage, but the president's "body man" was not so lucky. He was directly in the path of the regurgitations. As the elevator reached the floor where the ER was located, the trauma team turned in one direction and pointed the body man in another.

The president's color had gone from his usual spray tan burnt orange to a grayish, ashen ochre, giving the appearance of one who was experiencing severe jaundice. J.T. knew that the president famously claimed to have never taken a drink, but the claims of a politician could never be trusted, particularly this one. As the six attendants lifted the leviathan from the gurney to the table, J.T. barked orders to his team.

The team began to loosen the president's clothing over the president's objections. At one point he sat up and demanded that his body man be brought in. Calmly explaining that the emergency room was for medical personnel only, J.T. pushed the president back down on the table. The president grabbed the doctor by the collar of his scrubs and pulled him close to his face.

"What goes on here stays here, right?" the president growled.

"Of course," J.T. responded, freeing himself from the man's grip.

As the nurse loosened the president's belt and pulled down his pants, J.T. could see the reason for the executive's concern. The leader of the free world wore diapers, and this one was full. Taking but a second to translate *body man* to *diaper changer* in his head, J.T. encouraged the nurse to make quick work of it. Any number of diagnoses could explain the president's lack of continence, but J.T. suspected the rumors of severe cocaine or Adderall abuse played a part.

The largest threat to the sanitary conditions cleaned, blood was drawn, and a Foley catheter was inserted to extract urine. J.T.'s surgical mask hid the slight grin he displayed when the supine president howled in pain and indignation.

The team had placed a nitroglycerin pill in the president's mouth when he first arrived. The pill would work to relax the blood vessels and increase the supply of blood and oxygen to what J.T. was convinced was a fat-encased heart. While reducing the workload on the heart, the pill would also decrease the pain felt in the chest area. The quelling of the angina would allow the team to look at other areas of concern. With the obvious bowel problem, several issues came to mind, but none of them would present as acute as this crisis had.

J.T. poked the president's stomach in specific spots to locate the malady. Sharp abdominal pain might be a result of too much caviar and champagne or gas. There was also the possibility of appendicitis, gallstones, or a blockage of the intestines. It would take a few hours to rule out kidney stones, pancreatitis, or other serious issues. While J.T. poked, he could see that the nitroglycerin and Versed drip were doing their work. The president was lying quietly on the table, and his snarl had turned to a mumble.

J.T. knew that they were skirting into a Constitutional area that would have to be addressed sooner rather than later. If the president was going to be under sedation, the Twenty-Fifth Amendment to the Constitution might have to be invoked, and presidential power would be turned over to the vice president. Congress and the Cabinet would have to be notified. Minutes after becoming vice president, James C. "Whitey" Halfpenny might be placed in the position of taking the reins of power from his Republican primary opponent.

J.T.'s patient probing found what he believed to be the culprit in the lower right side of the president's prodigious belly. The doctor located the area after pushing aside a layer of fat that would have made an Iowa state fair prize-winning sow proud. While the pressing of the area drew a sharp breath from the president, the release of the pressure emitted a howl and a long stream of curse words. The Secret Service agent standing in the corner of the room stepped quicky to the table as if to get between the president and an assassin. J.T. stepped back but drew the agent to him.

"I'm going to need you to relay the information that the president has a burst appendix, and we need to do emergency surgery right now," J.T. whispered in the agent's ear. "We need to transfer the power of the president to the vice president before we put the president under."

The agent left the room immediately to notify others while J.T. went to the head of the operating table. "Mr. President, I have some bad news for you. You won't be attending any balls tonight," J.T. said. "I suspect you've been having some discomfort for the last couple of days. You probably chalked it up to one too many rubber-chicken dinners, but I'm afraid it's not." J.T. leaned in closer. "I'm afraid your appendix has burst, and we need to remove it right away."

The president's eyes hardened. "What—what are you talking about? I'm not going to let you cut me open. Where's my regular doctor? He'll tell you I'm as fit as a fiddle."

"I'm sure he would, Mr. President, but you're not fit," J.T. countered. "Right now, the poison from your appendix is spreading through your body. If we leave this untreated, it's going to lead to sepsis and possibly death. Actually, I'd say a man in your condition will certainly die."

At that moment the Secret Service agent came back into the ER with the vice president and another unidentified person. The stranger was carrying a clipboard with a document attached. J.T. moved behind the president's head so he could observe what was being presented.

The document read, *I am about to undergo surgery during which time I will be briefly and temporarily incapable of discharging the Constitutional powers and duties of the Office of the President of the United States.*

"I'm not signing this," President Taint said to the room.

The unidentified man responded, "As chief justice it will be my duty to report to the Cabinet and certain members of Congress that you have lost the ability to make clear decisions for yourself and the country. They will undoubtedly propose harsher measures than just a temporary abdication. We have already had the vice president sign his release of the powers back to you upon your successful surgery."

The chief justice flourished the document for the president. With assistance, the president rose enough to sign his skyscraper imitation signature to the document. Exhausted, he flopped back on the table. The vice president and chief justice left the room, and J.T. returned to the side of the operating table.

"Now let's see if we can clean out some of the poison that fills your body," J.T. said as he nodded at the anesthesiologist. "It'll all be over before you know it."

President Taint's face twisted into a quizzical expression as if he was thinking, *I wonder what he means by that?*

The anesthesiologist started his administration of propofol and spoke the timeworn phrase, "I'd like for you to count back for me from one hundred."

The anesthesiologist was not the only one in attendance who wondered whether the president could perform the task even while unmedicated.

~ ~ ~

David James Taint was born to a life of privilege in the upper echelon of Chicago society. The entire Gold Coast was visible from the family's four-thousand-square-foot penthouse. Little David's father had taken the advice of his own father and poured all the family's resources into real estate. David's grandfather had migrated to America from Europe to escape his homeland's compulsory military service.

"Serving in the army is for people too stupid to find a better way," Granddaddy Fred used to counsel his progeny.

Granddaddy Fred had made his fortune following goldminers across the US and Canada. It was his mission to provide the goldminers with whatever their recreational needs entailed. Whiskey, drugs, women—it didn't matter. Granddaddy Fred was a businessman whose sole purpose was to make his fortune in America and return a rich man to his homeland.

Ironically, when he returned to his homeland, he was denied entrance because he was a convicted draft dodger. Even his riches could not buy Granddaddy Fred's way back into the country of his birth. He returned to America and settled in Chicago, where he pursued his forays into the lodging industry.

Fred Jr. took over the reins and expanded the family's real estate a hundredfold. By all accounts he was a real estate genius who did not share his father's proclivities for the wild side. Fred Jr. understood the importance of making friends in high places and not allowing personal beliefs to get in the way of running a successful business.

His one slipup was being arrested in a Klan rally. He participated to protest what he considered was the ever-growing menace of Blacks moving north and taking jobs from their white counterparts. After his arrest he realized that the Klan was always violently opposed to the Jewish community. It was that Jewish community that Fred Jr. was dependent on to finance his real estate holdings. He never voiced his feelings about his heritage or disparaged other groups in public again. In private, it was a different matter.

In the 1970s, Taint Properties was sued by the federal government for discrimination in renting their apartment units. Whether the policy of not renting to people of color was exclusively the father's idea is not known. What is known is that investigators from the government determined that Taint Properties discriminated against potential renters of color. The Taints paid their fine, amended their behavior for a while, and continued business. Fred Jr. had the roadmap to success and was not going to let a little speed bump deter him in his path.

As successful as his business life was, his family life was a disaster. His oldest child, a daughter, chose to go into the legal profession. She resigned her judgeship due to tax improprieties and retired in dishonor. Fred Jr.'s second child, a son, hated him with a white-hot passion and refused to go into the family business. He died too early from alcoholism.

The youngest child, now the most important man in the world, was a miscreant from early on. A constant bully, he boasted about hitting a teacher in elementary school in his biography. Unable to control the child, the Taints did what so many families of that time did: they sent their child to a military school. Did the family realize the irony in seeing the grandson of a draft dodger pictured in a military uniform for most of his formative years?

Using the time-honored method of making large donations, the elder Taint was able to secure a place for his youngest son at a prestigious university. Continued donations managed to keep the student academically viable even though he was later described by one professor as "the dumbest student I've ever had."

Lacking any prospects of earning a living on his own, David James joined his father in the real estate game. While the father preferred to acquire wealth by purchasing rental properties, the son wanted to go after the big splashy purchases. The son's natural inclination was to grab as big a piece of property as the bank would extend them credit for. In his mind, he thought it important to have as many headlines as possible for every project he was involved in. To the heir, there was no bad publicity if David James Taint's name and picture were in the headlines.

Time after time, Fred Taint had to bail his son out of bad investments. It was as though the son's one true calling was making bad deals. To Fred's credit, he managed to keep his son's failures out of the headlines.

Ironically, it was said that Fred delighted in seeing the pictures of his son hobnobbing with the rich and famous. Perhaps he wanted the notoriety for himself but lacked the social skills to feel comfortable doing it. The escapades of his immigrant father were another consideration when Fred considered trying to join the blue bloods at civic events. Fred was happy to stay quietly in the background, allowing his son to bask in the limelight while buying and bullying his way into the upper echelons of Chicago society.

The pleasure his father felt was nothing compared to the pleasure David James felt as he squired model after model to the hottest clubs and parties. He was a man without a conscience, and some said consciousness. A biographer wrote that David James "lacked an ounce of curiosity and had the attention span of a nine-year-old with ADHD."

It was suspected that the drug known for raising mental acuity was abused during Donald James's partying years to the point of creating long-term stomach issues. Stomach issues that might require adult diapers. Stomach issues that might require a "body man" to take care of the embarrassing situation.

Before his stomach was compromised, David James traveled the world in search of the "perfect deal." He visited Moscow in 1987 when relations with the Soviet Union were less than normalized. His stated purpose was to build the largest skyscraper in the world. The project never came to fruition, but a long-term relationship with the power brokers in what would become modern-day Russia were formed. Those relationships proved valuable to the future presidential candidate.

Time after time, David James was able to find the money to start or complete a development that American banks considered too risky. Bankers interviewed about the solvency of the Taint empire would only speak off record. Their cautionary tales told of situations where loaning any more money to David James might ruin the bank if he went bankrupt. In point of fact, Taint companies declared bankruptcy six times over the years. In spite of the bankruptcies and the abysmal performance of his companies, the future candidate was promoted in the press and television as "America's premier businessman."

~ ~ ~

The mystique of a powerful businessman was foisted on millions of Americans by a television show. The show was highly promoted on a major network, whose reputation ensured that the viewer was convinced they were watching reality.

Stories abound about the condition of the real offices of the Taint empire. The conditions were so outdated and run-down that the "reality" show had to build sets to make the business appear to be more successful than it really was. Millions and millions of Americans were fooled by the façade, and a generation of viewers were led to believe that David James had the golden touch. As a result of the show, Taint was considered by the multitude of his viewers to be a very successful businessman, a man who "knew how to get things done."

Once convinced, the general public had a hard time deconstructing the Taint illusion. Stories of improprieties with underage women, sexual assaults, mafia ties, tenant intimidation, and a fake university were scandals that rolled off Taint like water off a duck's back. His veneer was considered to be impenetrable and earned him the nickname of "Teflon Taint." It was this complete sham of a man, this complete illusion, whom the Republican party chose as their candidate.

The announcement of his candidacy came in a press conference where his bigotry was in full bloom. Attacking those less fortunate than himself and ignoring his own documented failings, he railed at length about immigration. "When Mexico sends its people, they're not sending their best. They're not sending you. They're not sending you. They're sending people that have lots of problems, and they're bringing those problems with us. They're bringing drugs. They're bringing crime. They're rapists. And some, I assume, are good people." The media didn't point out that what the candidate was focusing on were the same things Taint himself had been accused of.

The media decided to abdicate their responsibilities as arbiters of truth and took the election off in the interest of making a close race. Primary debates resembled a cage of primates flinging their poo at one another. The Republican field was no match for the schoolyard bully who slandered and defamed as easily as one breathes. A lifetime of never being held accountable freed him to attack his opponents with savage ferocity.

The general election was more of the same. Faced off against one of the most qualified presidential candidates of all time, Taint let his full misogyny flourish. In the televised debates he paced recklessly close behind the Democratic candidate. He loomed large behind the front runner when it was her turn to speak. Was the skulking to intimidate, was it the narcissistic desire to be in every picture, or both? The view presented to the electorate, who had been preconditioned by the years of his television show, was that Taint was the man in charge. Despite losing the popular vote by nearly three million votes, Taint was declared the man in charge by the Electoral College.

In the short time between the election and the inauguration, scandals were already being reported. The ties to Russia were irrefutable, the payments made to ex-girlfriends as hush money were irrefutable, the nepotism was irrefutable. Taint announced his intention to place family members with no more business being in the public trust than a fox has being in a chicken coop in high positions of the government. To any casual observer of the body politic, the nepotism was for one purpose:---to help the Taint family gain as much power and wealth as possible as quickly as possible. Like hogs at a trough, the Taint family intended to feed on the public largesse as long and as deeply as they could.

Appointing family members and cronies to positions of power had prevented Taint from filling several important staff positions, such as his new medical team. When Taint closed his eyes entering the netherworld of anesthesia, he saw a Black man peering at him intently. Even in his disoriented state, he knew fear. It was not the fear of the surgery's outcome; it was the fear of a Black man that was not in a servile position. The man looking back at him was daring to look Taint directly in the eye as an equal. The Black man was not afraid of Taint, and that created a deep visceral fear in Taint.

~ ~ ~

As J.T. looked at the result of decades of excess on the table before him, he paused for a brief second. He was looking down on a man without conscience. Whatever empathy Taint had been born with had been beaten out of him as a child by the military school's proctors or his father. Taint existed as a truly transactional character; his only concern was how a thing benefited him. If he didn't stand to gain from a transaction, it didn't interest him. There was not a shred of compassion for his fellow man in his three hundred and fifty pounds. Not a shred.

J.T. called, "Scalpel," and reached out his hand to receive the instrument. As he grasped it firmly, he had a flashback to an ethics class he had taken long ago. The question posed had been, *If you could go back in time and kill baby Hitler, would you?* The arguments in the classroom had become fierce at times, with both sides attempting to capture the moral high ground. J.T. had even used in his argument that a newspaper poll at the time reported that 42 percent of their respondents would indeed kill baby Hitler if time travel were possible.

In the end, the ethics professor pointed out to the would-be baby killers that baby Hitler was without sin. Baby Hitler had not committed genocide, or even shoplifted. The fact that one knew with certainty that someone was going to one day be a tyrant was not sufficient reason to take another's life. The professor used the term *moral injury* to describe the possible huge personal costs when one acted against their moral beliefs. "Don't kill children" is probably the deepest held moral belief of society. The professor argued that violating that most simple of norms could come at a severe emotional price for the rest of one's life.

J.T. shook his head as if to rattle the memory from his mind. What lay before him was not an ethical supposition. What lay before him was three hundred pounds of suet encasing the jet-black soul of an aspiring oligarch. There was not a doubt in J.T.'s mind that the termination of David James Taint's life would save thousands if not millions of lives. Whether it was by nuclear holocaust, or a more insidious holocaust that destroyed all the perceived enemies of the entitled white Anglo-Saxon protestant male one group at a time, J.T. was convinced that President-elect Taint was on a mission to cleanse the human race of all its "impurities." If the president made a few bucks along the way, well, so much the better.

J.T. made his initial cuts with the precision that had built his reputation as the best surgeon in the Army. He quickly removed the burst appendix and cleaned the abdominal cavity. A pocket of pus that had formed in the abdomen was removed. All the pockets of infection were cleaned, preventing an abscess. From the appendix J.T. moved to the gallbladder, which was swollen and hard to the touch. J.T. suspected the organ was full of stones and ordered an endoscopy.

"He's already out. Might as well give him the VIP treatment while we've got him," J.T. offered to the anesthesiologist.

The endoscope revealed years of scarring due to acid reflux and a gallbladder and bile duct full of stones. J.T. set about performing a cholecystectomy, the surgical removal of the gallbladder. As he pushed layers of fat out of the way he cursed the condition of the body he was being asked to perform on. There were no corpses being donated to medical schools with a BMI approaching the seventies. There were no soldiers in the field that were obese. J.T. was in uncharted waters.

The fact that Taint could still walk away from the inaugural podium without help was a testimony to the genes he had inherited from his explorer grandfather. As the president-elect lay on the operating table, completely exposed for the fraud that he was, J.T. flashed back to a moment in his youth. The moment that had defined him. J.T. held a dark secret in his heart that would have ruined his life forever if revealed. It was his secret—no one else knew—but if it had been revealed at any point in his life, he would have had to pay the consequences. He used that moment to drive himself to achieve, to rise as high as he could and to do as much good for others as he could.

The corpulent mass on the table chose the moment of J.T.'s reverie to twitch, which in a man his size was not a small movement. J.T. felt his scalpel dig a bit deeper than intended because of the movement. He was operating in a particularly dicey part of the anatomy, near where the vagus nerve attached to the intestine. His quick observation revealed no visible problems, and J.T. continued.

After nine hours the surgery was finally completed, and the leader of the free world was wheeled to the recovery room. Upon awaking, Taint's first words were, "Give me that letter back! Tell that SOB Whitey I'm back!" At which point he began to purge violently. The chief justice, who was extending the transfer-of-powers letter to the president, had to retract quickly to avoid the vomitus.

J.T. was called in and was shocked by the white-hot heat of rage from the man who could barely take a breath without purging. The president's eyes burned a hole through the doctor as he attempted to make his patient more comfortable.

If looks could kill, I'd be molding in my grave, J.T thought as he attempted to take the vitals of the flailing president. Ordering medications to soothe the nausea, J.T. watched for any signs of postoperative problems. The president didn't appear to be in any immediate danger. J.T had the president transferred to the one hospital room housed in the unit for overnight observation. Transferring Taint to Walter Reed was ruled out to minimize the effect of the president's illness on the markets and world stability. They had everything they needed at the WHMU, and J.T. wanted to stay on top of the case.

If Taint were transferred it would be the end of J.T.'s tenure in the White House. J.T. was sure his replacement was already on the way. Still, he wanted to tarry a bit longer, even if he had to incur the president's disdain to do it. He called his wife and explained the situation while cautioning her that everything was highly confidential.

"We can celebrate every day for the rest of our lives," J.T. whispered into his phone. "Right now, I need to stay on top of this."

"Sure, honey, you're right," came the reply. "The celebration dinner can wait. What you're doing is far more important. I'm so proud of you."

J.T hung up and went to the cafeteria, where he would camp out for most of the night. In his conscious mind he retraced his steps through the procedures, questioning every move. In his brief moments of sleep, he would slip into a nightmare that caused him to jerk awake as the nightmare was reaching its climax.

At six in the morning, he groggily made his way to the president's room. To his surprise the president was awake and surrounded by a gaggle of people, one of whom introduced himself as the president's personal physician. The man motioned for J.T. to follow him out into the hall.

Dr. Mark Bauer was a tall fair-skinned man of about sixty. He came right to the point. "I have ordered a gastroscopy to see if I can confirm my suspicion."

"Your suspicion. What is your suspicion?" J.T. queried.

"That our president has suffered gastroparesis," Dr. Bauer answered. "Knowing him to be a man whose stomach empties quite regularly, I suspect that his stomach has not restarted after surgery. We will have to wait for a day or so to confirm, but I believe I'm right."

J.T. let the suspicion sink in. From his medical training, J.T. knew that if true, the president was in for a lifetime of indigestion, bloated stomach, nausea, vomiting, heartburn, and constipation. As if to enter the conversation, the president regurgitated loudly from inside the room. Both doctors hurried to his side.

The president turned to his doctor. "You've got to fix this. Whatever he's done to me, you have to fix it. I can't be president and throwing up like a baby all the time. Who's going to fear me when I'm puking all the time?"

And he was right, and his doctor was right. The president did suffer from gastroparesis, and it did prevent him from performing his duties, to the point of having to resign. The doctor alluded to the onset of the condition as something that occurred during the gallbladder surgery. It was his opinion that the vagus nerve had been severed or disrupted. There was no way to know for sure without opening the president up again, and no one wanted to do that.

J.T. retired to his beloved West Virginia mountains, high atop a hill in his hometown, his ethics intact. For the first few months of his retirement, he replayed the operation frequently in his mind. Over time his recollections faded and his concern about the "ethical dilemma" vanished.

There is more than one way to prevent a tyrant.

ACKNOWLEDGEMENTS

First to my wife Karen who for forty plus years has stood beside me attempting to guide me in the right direction. Your encouragement and constant support have allowed me to achieve my dream of being an author. Thanks for aways being my best friend and allowing me to be me.

To my sons Christopher and Patrick, I can't say enough about the love, support, and encouragement you have shown while I have attempted to carve out a niche in the publishing world. You guys are the best sons any father could hope for and I look at my grandchildren with great pride knowing that good men are raising them.

Appreciation must be given to the people brave enough to withstand the horrors of reading someone else's novel. In my case they include Renee Hudson, and my brother John. Very special thanks go to Lila La Bine who edited the book into something that was readable. I wouldn't have made it without the finishing touches masterfully applied by Lila who continues to show me the intricacies of the English language with patience and good humor. Thanks must go out to the whole crew at Sandy Springs Press. Thank you all.